"This is a book for anyone who has ever asked, 'God, are you there?' Joseph Bentz helps us turn the question around so that the question becomes a declaration: 'God, you are everywhere!'"

—Dean Nelson
Professor, Point Loma Nazarene University
Author of *God Hides in Plain Sight:*
How to See the Sacred in a Chaotic World

"Joseph Bentz has a gift for seeing the Holy Spirit in ordinary places. Let this book open your eyes to the God who is at work all around you."

—Lawrence W. Wilson
Author of *When Life Doesn't Turn Out the Way You Expect* and
Why Me? Straight Talk about Suffering

"Joseph Bentz is right . . . sometimes it's *hard* to recognize the presence of God. In his insightful book, Joseph Bentz peels back the mystery surrounding why we overlook God's presence in our life, and more importantly, how we can recognize it. This book is a must for everyone who's ever longed to experience more of God."

—Donna Jones
Pastor's wife, national speaker
Author of *Seek: A Woman's Guide to Meeting God*

PIECES
of
HEAVEN

Recognizing the Presence of God

JOSEPH BENTZ

BEACON HILL PRESS
OF KANSAS CITY

ISBN 978-0-8341-2886-6

Printed in the
United States of America

Cover Design: Arthur Cherry
Inside Design: Sharon Page

Library of Congress Cataloging-in-Publication Data

Bentz, Joseph, 1961-
   Pieces of heaven : recognizing the presence of God / Joseph Bentz.
      p. cm.
   Includes bibliographical references.
   ISBN 978-0-8341-2886-6 (pbk.)
   1. Presence of God   2. God—Knowableness.   3. God (Christianity)—Omnipresence.   I. Title.
      BT180.P6B46 2012
      248.2—dc23

                                                          2012020368

10 9 8 7 6 5 4 3 2 1

CONTENTS

one ⊠ ⊠ ⊠
THE THIN PLACE
IN THE VEIL

■ God doesn't behave the way I wish He would.

Even though I've been a Christian for many years, I still have a hard time explaining to someone who is not a believer why I can't help but be a follower of Jesus Christ. It's not that I lack the words to describe the doctrine or to tell the story of how God got hold of me. But how do I describe God's powerful but invisible presence that keeps pulling me toward Him?

It would be easier if God chose to be more visible and obvious about how He inserts himself into people's lives. I would love to be able to say, "I am a Christian because God appeared above my house in the form of a radiant fireball and summoned me outside. In view of all my neighbors, who recorded the whole thing, He declared (in a booming voice, of course) that Jesus Christ is the way to salvation and that I should follow Him."

When Hollywood portrays God, they often do it in this more readily grasped, visual way. Who comes to mind when you think of a Hollywood-created God? A kindly, cigar-smoking George Burns? The wise and unflappable

Morgan Freeman? Or maybe you prefer it when the special effects kick in and you get something like the God of *Raiders of the Lost Ark*.[1]

Do you remember how the presence of God is portrayed in that movie? The Nazis want the ark of the covenant because they think they can use the power of God's presence in it for their own evil purposes. When they finally get the ark, they lift up the lid and watch as bright white waves of smoke rise up from the box. The light swirls round and round, dozens of ribbons of it flying high in the air, with awe-inspiring beauty and power. Then majestic columns of fire rise from the ark and extend high into the air. The Nazis are triumphant.

But then, because God is apparently smart enough to know that these guys are Nazis and therefore bad guys, the whole scene turns ugly for them. The fire forms into huge daggers that stab right through the center of the soldiers' bodies and kill them.

But that punishment is only for the low-ranking Nazi soldiers. The top Nazis suffer an even worse fate. The heads of the two leaders begin to melt, and they scream in pain. As if that were not gruesome enough, the head of the most villainous, whiny-voiced Nazi leader explodes in blood and gore like a smashed watermelon. Then all the fire and smoke come together in one gigantic column that shoots high above the island. Finally it collapses back down into the ark with a tremendous slam of the lid.

Beautiful. Smoke and fire and melting heads. That may not fit everyone's concept of God's presence, but at least it's something people can see and understand.

In my own life, the Holy Spirit doesn't work that way. He is not flash and spectacle. He is not a booming voice. Nor is

He a crusty but affable old man. He is not anything a Hollywood camera could capture.

He is a loving, abiding presence. More than anything else, I am a Christian because of God's powerful, pursuing Spirit. As Romans 8:16 says, "The Spirit himself testifies with our spirit that we are God's children." I can also discuss my faith in terms of doctrine and theology and biblical principles, but God's *presence* is what keeps me tied to the faith even through crises of doubt, discouragement, and my own failures. How can I describe that presence? It's the most important part of my faith, but it's also the hardest to talk about and the easiest for skeptics to dismiss.

The idea for this book was sparked by an overheard conversation about the presence of God. It was a simple moment, but I couldn't get it out of my mind. As my friends in the Christian writers group that was meeting in my home were getting ready to leave, I walked into the kitchen to hear one of our members, Lynn, speaking to another member of the group. She was describing a recent worship service she had been part of in which the people powerfully sensed the presence of the Holy Spirit. She said it was one of those times when the veil between us and eternity seemed very thin and almost disappeared. I can still picture the way she held her palms together as she said this, as if she were touching this thin, almost transparent barrier that she was describing.

That thin place in the veil is what this book is about.

God is always with us, I believe, but often the barriers are so thick—because of noise, disbelief, indifference, daily responsibilities, and other distractions—that we find ourselves paying little attention to Him. He is easy to ignore. Popular entertainment mocks Him, the political world is wary of Him, much of the intellectual elite denies Him, and a frenzied online social media loses Him in a flurry of trivia. It's easy to leave God out of our conversations and thoughts—at work, at school, in social settings, and unfortunately sometimes even at church. How can we open our eyes to His presence?

This book will consider "God in the ordinary" and "God in the extraordinary." In the ordinary His Spirit is powerfully present in music, in nature, in the intellect, in prayer, and in Scripture. We may find God's presence in our relationships, not only with those we love but also in those who cause us problems.

In the extraordinary He also manifests himself at rare times in more unusual ways, in powerful revivals, in people's encounters with angels, or in the moments before death.

I wish reaching the thin places was all in our own power, but it isn't. As this book will explore, God reveals and conceals His presence in His own timing for His own purposes, as He has always done. The temptation, when God seems distant, is to fill the space with a counterfeit god. You don't even have to choose one—the god will choose you. Many people are worshiping multiple counterfeit gods right now without even knowing it.

I wrote this book because I want to do all I can to strip away the barriers that hide God's presence. I long to get as close as I can to the thin place in the veil that my friend was describing.

If you long for that too—for a deeper connection with the Holy Spirit—then I ask you to join me in these pages.

two ☒ ☒ ☒
STAMPING OUT GOD

Do not quench the Spirit.
—1 Thessalonians 5:19

■ What does it take to quench the Spirit of God? Can governments do it by banning displays of the Ten Commandments from public places? Can they do it by ordering public prayer and other religious expressions out of classrooms? Can celebrity scientists do it by declaring that God doesn't exist? Can Christians do it by withdrawing into an individualistic faith that refuses to find God's Spirit in the poor and oppressed people they should be serving? Can popular culture do it by treating Christ and His followers with mockery in films, television shows, and music—if those entertainers bother to acknowledge God's existence at all?

All these Spirit-quenching forces are worth considering, but I want to start with one that is much simpler. It doesn't take a Supreme Court decision or a derisive anti-Christian television show to push my thoughts away from God. I can do that all by myself. Spiritual indifference quenches the Spirit more than all the powers of government and pop culture on earth.

I don't *want* to quench the Spirit, but I do it all the time. So does the world I live in. Why?

The greatest moments of my life have been times when I have sensed the soul-shaking power of God's presence so intensely that I was overwhelmed with joy. But I have to admit that even though I am a committed Christian and would like to think that I would die for my faith if necessary, I spend much of my time not thinking about God at all.

Why would a believer like me, who really does love God and who really does know what it is like to celebrate His loving presence, not do everything he can to contemplate Him and commune with Him as often as possible?

I do that—sometimes. But then my concentration drifts to other things, and in my distraction or anger or enthusiasm I shut Him out of my thoughts altogether. Unfortunately, I don't always operate in a way that leads me to focus on things that are most important. My mind often latches onto what is trivial but immediate rather than what is profound but distant.

For instance, if you want to get my attention, especially when I'm hungry, describe to me a hot pizza with a crispy, delicate crust at its base, covered with cheese so thick and gooey that as I pull out my slice from the rest of the pizza, white slivers of it hang down. Tell me about the sausage and pepperoni and mushrooms on top, and remind me of the pleasure of that first hot bite. I want that pizza.

Or you could set off my hunger pangs with a hot fudge sundae. Make me see that lumpy hot chocolate sauce flowing over the cold vanilla ice cream and cascading to the bottom of the cup. Sprinkle on some nuts, some whipped cream, and a cherry on top, and I can't wait to dig in.

But now tell me you want to sweep aside thoughts of trivial matters like pizza slices and hot fudge sundaes. Instead, ask me to contemplate something important, something that will matter not only for the duration of one meal but *forever*. Tell me to think about the face of God. Ask me to consider that as a Christian, my future includes *eternity* in God's presence, in a paradise beyond my imagination.

That should thrill me, right?

In a certain sense it does. But even though I'm a passionate Christian, and even though I spend a good portion of my days *writing* about Christian issues and contemplating scripture and praying, hearing about "the face of God" and eternity leaves me a little flat. It feels pretty distant unless I'm in just the right frame of mind.

How Did *God* Get Deleted from the Conversation?

The world in which we live makes it easy to ignore God. He gets pushed away from us not just by one force or distraction but by many. Take our everyday conversations. The social etiquette of our day reinforces the habit of pushing God away. Think of the many places and situations in which any mention of God is considered rude, inappropriate, or even illegal. For most people, God is left out of large swaths of their social life, business dealings, time in public schools, and to a greater extent than most would like to admit, their discussions at church. I am not referring here primarily to the more controversial legal prohibitions against public displays of religion, although those may play a role. But even informally, where religious discussions are allowed, many often avoid them anyway. People in business settings don't want to give offense to coworkers or clients who may have religious beliefs that differ from their own, so they avoid the subject of religion. Neighbors at a block party or parents at a little league game may know little or nothing about the spiritual lives of these acquaintances, so they stay away from this subject that might offend.

Even if you agree that it's a good idea to avoid spiritual discussions in such settings, think of what a big chunk of life is now excluded from any talk of God. The desire to dodge awkward religious misunderstandings and avoid offense becomes a far more powerful force in quenching the Spirit than any stated policy or law.

The public school my children attend, for instance, is not hostile to Christianity exactly, but the school treats it as something about which everyone should remain politely silent. A social studies class may devote a unit to Christianity, just as it includes short studies of Islam and Buddhism, but these religions are treated as historical and cultural topics with little relevance to the students' daily lives.

The one social gathering place where you might expect robust conversations about God to still be taking place is the church. Those discussions do happen, but even there, politeness often overshadows deep engagement in spiritual issues. In an era in which denominational lines are breaking down and community churches attract members of ever-widening arrays of beliefs, people are more careful not to raise sensitive theological issues that may cause offense.

This diversity of theological assumptions, rather than becoming an opportunity for vigorous conversations about the disputed issues, instead becomes a reason for avoiding those controversies altogether. Better to have a vague or dumbed-down theology that the congregation can agree on than to risk alienating people by challenging their beliefs or asking them to carefully examine them.

Because people in the church become so used to downplaying spiritual discussions in other settings—work, social occasions, school—that reticence spills over into church relationships. People who are not used to talking about spiritual issues often prefer to keep quiet about them because they're a little fuzzy about those beliefs themselves and certainly wouldn't want to be put on the spot to explain them. They also don't want to risk complicating a relationship at church over religion any more than they would want to do so at work or among fellow parents of their children's soccer league. Except for the formal religious services themselves, church too often becomes, ironically enough, a religion-free discussion zone where conversations are not all that much different from what they would be anywhere else.

Why People Choose Faith-Suppressing Silence

Why are people so inclined to shut God out of their conversations (even at church), when so many thousands of other topics are easy to talk about? Why do people worry about offending others with differences of opinion in areas of faith while other differences of opinion are not so sensitive?

One reason, I believe, is that people almost never *fully* trust what other people say about their experience of God. One's relationship with God strikes at something so personal and deep that people don't want to treat it lightly, especially among listeners who might misunderstand. Words are so limited that it is difficult for many to describe their connection to the Lord. In the right circumstances they might share it, but only in those rare situations in which they feel free to probe things that are most important to them.

Believers trying to express their relationship with God come to expect skepticism, if not condescension or even outright hostility, from many listeners. With so many instances of so-called Christians trying to *use* God for their own purposes, misquoting scripture, not living up to their faith with their actions, and other human failures, sincere believers have trouble not being lumped in with hypocrites. Knowing they will have to face this barrier of suspicion if they discuss the relationship that is most important to them, they learn to keep it to themselves for the most part. In time, they may learn not to discuss it at all. Surrounded by other mostly silent Christians, their faith itself may begin to fade.

In some earlier eras, God was harder to ignore than He is today. As a teacher of American literature, I have spent many hours steeped in the writings of the Puritan era. While there was certainly danger and corruption in some of the beliefs and actions of the people at that time, one thing you have to say for it is that it was a God-drenched age. People talked about Him and prayed to Him. Sermon collections were bestsellers. In their spare time people read those sermons to one other. Their poetry was about God. Their songs were about God. Their celebrities were pastors, not athletes or actors as in our own generation.

This concentration on God didn't guarantee that individuals believed in Him sincerely or that they always behaved with integrity. They had the choice, as we do, to truly follow God or not. But at least in that era, more than ours, they couldn't as easily simply *ignore* God. They had to come to terms with Him. In our day it is much easier for people to dismiss Him from the outset without ever contemplating Him much at all.

Another difference between the culture most of us live in today and earlier God-drenched eras is that we are more likely to compartmentalize our spiritual lives in ways that confine God to certain small "religious" spaces and exclude Him from the rest of our experience. I recently read Tim Stafford's book *Surprised by Jesus*, in which he makes the point that the people of Jesus' day didn't make as much distinction as we do between the natural and the supernatural.

God created and controls the universe, they believed, and His hand is seen in everything that happens. Most of the time God chooses to have the world work in certain ways, and you could call those ways natural "laws" if you like, but occasionally He alters that usual way of doing things and performs a portent or sign. It is all God. He can do whatever He wants. For them, God was not confined to only the "religious" parts of life the way He is for so many people in our day. They saw His presence and influence all over the place: in worship, in Scripture, in nature, in each other.

People of that era so intertwined the natural and supernatural that they didn't even use the word "miracle" in the New Testament. Instead, Stafford says, "Jesus did 'wonders' (*paradoxa*), 'acts of power' (*dunameis*), 'signs' (*semeia*) or 'portents' (*terata*). None of these words lends itself to the God-against-nature distinction. All these words can be applied perfectly well to a sunrise or a storm, which are everyday parts of nature, just as well as to a healing."[1] For us a miracle is a deviation from the laws of nature, but for them it was simply a decision by the Creator of those "laws" to do something a little differently this time.

Taking God Off the Table from the Start

In those more religious eras, the existence of God and the importance and validity of faith as a way to understand life were taken as starting points. For many people today, the opposite is true. God is taken off the table from the start. It is simply assumed that faith in God plays no part in understanding reality or making sense of it. He is deleted not only from personal conversations but also in significant ways from the *cultural* conversation.

Science, or at least a certain narrow conception of it, has emerged for many as the god of modern thought. It is a view of science that takes as a starting point the conviction that everything is here without purpose or design, without a God who created the universe. It is a science that is therefore suspicious of traditional ideas of the "soul" or "mind." It discards or minimizes the validity not only of religion to answer the important questions of life but also of other ways of understanding that have served us for millennia, such as art, literature, and music. People who hold this view decide that nothing supernatural exists. Matter is all there is, and everything in the universe can be explained by natural processes. No need for God—He can be ejected from the conversation.

That approach certainly simplifies things. If the supernatural does not exist, then not only can God be set aside, but concepts such as "soul" or "mind" can be reduced to nothing more than chemical or biological processes. Even the idea of a "self" that exists apart from a physical body, a self that transcends the physical, a self that is more than a collection of matter behaving a certain way, is essentially an illusion. Is the "self" that I believe is me real, or is it merely a trick of the sophisticated interaction and activity of the chemicals and other matter in my brain? Will that "me" cease to exist as soon as the physical processes of that brain cease to function?

It's a crucial question, one that artists, preachers, poets, and theologians have grappled with for millennia. But if the possibility of the supernatural, of God, is swept aside, then those people have been questioning in vain. To accept scientific naturalism means to reject or radically redefine many other things our intuition may tell us are true. Intuition itself, for instance, must be illusory, some kind of chemical brain process. Religion, love, art, and literature aren't really the expressions of a yearning soul as Christians and lovers and artists have deluded themselves into believing.

Marilynne Robinson laments this narrow view of reality in her book *Absence of Mind*. How, for instance, would those who hold this worldview answer the question *What is art?* Robinson writes, "It is a means of attracting mates, even though artists may have felt that it was an exploration of experience, of the possibilities of communication, and of the extraordinary collaboration of eye and hand." The artist, in this view, is self-deceived. "Leonardo and Rembrandt may have thought they were competent inquirers in their own right, but we moderns know better."[2]

Robinson argues for putting the mind—and religion and art and intuition and the soul—back on the table as ways of understanding reality. Scientific naturalism has tried to reinterpret—or explain away—the Holy Spirit or love or Shakespeare or Beethoven or Ecclesiastes. Its practitioners have overreached. Let science explain what it can, but don't exclude other legitimate ways of knowing.

One of the top scientists of our day, Francis Collins, who was the head of the Human Genome Project, which mapped the three-billion-letter DNA code of our species, agrees that science simply can't explain everything. He writes, "Science's domain is to explore nature. God's domain is in the spiritual world, a realm not possible to explore with the tools and language of science. It must be examined with the heart, the mind, and the soul—and the mind must find a way to embrace both realms."[3]

Instead, our culture has allowed science to become the primary authority on questions outside its domain and has marginalized or stifled the legitimacy of the heart, mind, and soul as a way of understanding reality. A false opposition has emerged between science and faith, when in fact there is no reason they cannot work in harmony. Collins asserts that "there is no conflict in being a rigorous scientist and a person who believes in a God who takes a personal interest in each one of us. . . . But science is powerless to answer questions such as 'Why did the universe come into being?' 'What is the meaning of human existence?' 'What happens after we die?'"[4]

The problem is not simply that some scientists *disagree* with the Christian beliefs on these issues but that the issues are so often considered settled before they are even raised. As Dallas Willard has described our culture's dismissive stance toward faith, "The world 'taken for granted' by generations past, and still by many contemporary Christians in America today, can no longer be taken seriously by decent, intelligent people. The Apostle's Creed is on a level with the flat earth. So it is often assumed now."[5]

These assumptions have become so powerful in our generation that they have pushed some Christians into Spirit-quenching timidity. Scientific ideas are welcomed for public discussion. "Religious" ideas are expected to be kept not only private but also silent. Even in discussions among Christians themselves, I find a reluctance to assert too much about their experiences in the realm of faith. Intuition, communion with God, prayer, sensing God's presence—these topics are considered purely "personal," too risky to say too much about.

To make matters worse, some Christians have crippled their own vocabularies when it comes to talking about spiritual issues. The trend among many Christians is to avoid theological and spiritual terms altogether, even in the rare occasions when they do discuss religious issues with non-believers. Those words are considered insider language or "Christianese" and are thought to be offensive or confusing to those outside the faith. I understand the need to explain terms and not to use language to exclude people, but the trend away from using traditional theological terms has gone so far that many Christians hardly have a language at all.

Why not use terms like "salvation" and "atonement" and "sanctification" with one another and with those not in our faith, but probe their meaning together? Better to use insider language with frank discussion to go along with it than to stay silent. Everywhere I go I am confronted by the language of other realms of thought—medicine, sports, video games, electronics technology. The people who inhabit those areas of interest don't dumb down their language for me or refuse to use their terminology for fear of confusing me or offending me. If I don't understand, I ask, and they explain.

Living in Denial of the Big Things, Like Death

When I look at my own behavior as a Christian, I'm bothered that it's so easy for God to slip out of my conversation and my thoughts so much of the time. How can I keep quiet about something so big? If I were really committed to God, wouldn't I find it impossible *not* to talk about Him more often? Why do trivial issues—the latest celebrity trial, the upcoming sports event, a perceived insult from a colleague—grip my mind and easily push out things that are far more worth thinking about? Like most people I know, I end up living in denial of big things much of the time, especially big things that have significant spiritual implications.

Take death. People of all political beliefs, religions, nationalities, and classes believe in it, but people in all those groups also live much of their lives in denial of it. My friend Monica Ganas analyzes our culture's denial of death in her book *Under the Influence*. She points out the many ways we deny death both before it arrives and even after it comes. The first response we have to death, understandably, is to try to keep it from happening. Entire industries are set up to hold death off, even though the word itself is seldom used. Ganas writes, "I am expected to hope that if I jog long enough, or purchase the right vitamins, or hold out for the right stem cell research, or reduce the stress in my life (the stress of grief), I might postpone the death issue indefinitely."[6]

Even when someone does die, our culture still finds ways to minimize that reality. When Ganas, who has worked in the Hollywood entertainment industry, attended the memorial service of her former manager, she deeply felt the need to gather with family and friends to grieve the loss of a man who had been such a strong influence in her life. Instead, the "celebration of life" (note the denial of death in that description of the service) turned into a string of "performances" by his friends and former clients, many of them stand-up comics, who turned the event into "nonstop entertainment, with bands playing and occasional dancing." Grief was banished, the reality of death was denied, and happiness was the tone imposed on an event that became a venue for self-promotion and networking.[7]

Our cultural practices deny death in many ways. Families have little contact with the loved one's body after death. Professionals carefully prepare the body with makeup and other techniques to minimize the harsh reality of death. Funerals are kept upbeat and celebratory. People rarely wear black anymore as a sign of mourning. Coffins, which often used to be buried in graveyards right next to the church as frequent reminders of the fleeting nature of life, now are buried in cemeteries that are farther away and rarely visited. Ancient churches themselves used to serve as a kind of coffin, with the dead buried under the floors and in the walls. Church members could see the names of these deceased Christians and be reminded not only of their own mortality but also of the fact that new members were building on a foundation that stretched back generations. Today, dead Christians are taken away and buried where their names may rarely if ever be heard again.

I recently read an article in which a pastor complained that there were not enough funerals in his church. While that may sound like a good problem, Pastor Todd Friesen said the infrequency of funerals stunts the congregation's spiritual formation. A funeral teaches people how to "measure their days."[8] A person's life on earth will end. Might a more realistic awareness of mortality lead a church member to live life better and more fully? Would a church member who attends a funeral of a long-time Christian and hears memories of how that person served others or was a good parent be more likely to reflect on the priorities in his or her own life? These opportunities are missed as older congregants move to retirement communities and have their memorial services conducted away from the churches where younger members could take part in the review of a long life that a funeral provides.

Earlier generations were reminded of death more frequently even among animals. My mother told me of her grandmother wringing a chicken's neck in the backyard before preparing to cook it. Her generation observed death in this way as a routine aspect of everyday life. My own children would be horrified to contemplate the thought that the little chicken nuggets they dip into their barbecue sauce had anything to do with such a killing process.

Although some people approach the Bible as a book of stilted, stained-glass prose, Scripture takes a more frank outlook on death than our generation does. My regular Scripture reading recently took me through a particularly

stomach-turning section of Leviticus. I read of a bull being killed and its blood splattered around in a certain way.
I read of its liver and its kidney and other entrails, not to
mention the dung. I stopped reading and tried to imagine
how the congregation at my own church would react if we
still had to perform such rituals. Right now the closest we
get to any physical representation of death is tiny cups of
grape juice and polite little wafers. Actual blood and guts
would no doubt send many church members screaming
from the sanctuary, but the people back then knew death.
They saw it, understood it, and had to contemplate it in all
its graphic reality.

Setting Aside Denial, Embracing the Truth

Some may ask, *Why not deny death, or at least find ways to
minimize its gruesome impact? Since death is such an unpleasant
reality, isn't it better to ignore it until you absolutely have to face
it?* Coming to terms with death means facing other difficult realities and huge questions that many people prefer
to avoid. One reality is that in the scheme of history, not to
mention eternity, life is fleeting. I do not live on this earth
very long. Every second of the day I am racing toward the
end of this earthly existence. Why am I here for this short
span? Why am I here at all? Does my existence have meaning? Is it an accident? Did God create me? If so, does He love
me? Is it possible to know Him? What do I believe about
eternity? Is death the end, or does something come after it?
If something comes after, then how can I be ready for it?

Death wakes us up to life's significance. But our culture
in its denial of death, urges, *Stay asleep to those harsh questions. Enjoy yourself! Don't think about what happens after, or
if you do, give these questions only the most cursory attention.
Develop a quick little philosophy that dismisses the questions, per-*

haps with irony or sarcasm, and then move on. Focus on the here and now so much that such ultimate questions fade away. Focus on making more money. Build up the retirement account, trade in the old car for a newer one. Entertain yourself. Lose yourself in fun and work and projects. If the big questions come up, make fun of them. You'll forget about them again soon enough.

Christians believe that death doesn't end our existence but instead leads us to an eternity of joy in God's presence. But do we live as if we are essentially in denial of that truth? Not long ago I taught a series for my adult Sunday school class on Randy Alcorn's book *Heaven*. As Alcorn himself writes, the hardest part of teaching about heaven is getting people to care about it. Heaven is our destination, but how much time do Christians spend studying what Scripture has to say about it or imagining what it will be like? Alcorn points out that many people may never have heard a sermon on heaven: "We're told how to *get* to Heaven, and that it's a better place than Hell, but we're taught remarkably little about Heaven itself."[9]

Why such neglect of a place that is not only such an important part of our future but that in the grand scheme of eternity is part of our *very near* future? One excuse people give is that we *can't* know much about it because the Bible doesn't reveal much. But Alcorn, in a five-hundred-page book, shows that Scripture reveals that our eternal home is not the heaven of stereotype. It is not a disembodied place of clouds and harps and floating angels. Instead, the new earth will be a *physical* realm, in which we will have bodies. Heaven will contain gardens and cities and buildings and banquets and music and friendship and fun. Many Christians know that 1 Corinthians 2:9 says, "'No eye has seen . . . no ear has heard . . . no human mind has conceived'— the things God has prepared for those who love him," but they neglect the following verse, which adds, "these are the things God has revealed to us by his Spirit" (verse 10).

Although heaven is obviously beyond our comprehension in some ways, and while we know there will be many surprises, what prevents us from spending more time dwelling on what we *do* know about it from Scripture, or *imagining* what it might be from hints that are given? Alcorn raises the possibilities of travel to distant planets, the creation of new works of music and art and literature, the enjoyment of sports and play, reunions with old friends and the creation of new friendships with the great figures of history—all of which are compatible with Scripture's view of heaven. But do most of us spend any time thinking about this, even as much time as we would spend anticipating an upcoming vacation here on earth?

Alcorn waits a long time—until chapter 17—before he finally explores what he considers the most important part of heaven, which is that we will see God and live with Him forever. Why does he take so long to get to that part? He writes, "If I were dealing with aspects of Heaven in their order of *importance*, I would have begun with a chapter about God and our eternal relationship with him." The reason he doesn't start with that is that the whole idea of "beholding God's face" has been "poisoned by dull stereotypes and vague, lifeless caricatures." He adds, "To see God's face is the loftiest of all aspirations—though sadly, for most of us, it's not at the top of our wish list. (If we understand what it means, it will be.)"[10]

Death. Heaven. Seeing God's face. Living in God's presence. Important realities. I embrace each one, but I also know they may get crowded out by more urgent thoughts—getting to work on time, seeing the final episode of my favorite television show, winning the argument with my wife, seeing my friends' latest Facebook posts.

Is there a way to change my life so that I break free of denial and triviality more often? What can I do to more carefully attune myself to the reality of God's presence? The next chapter will consider those questions.

Go to beaconhillbooks.com for a free downloadable study guide that includes questions for deeper personal reflection as well as activities for use in a small-group setting.

three ☒ ☒ ☒
WAKING UP TO GOD'S PRESENCE

■ One person who tried an experiment in shutting out the trivia of life in order to focus more on God was Frank C. Laubach, a missionary in the Philippines in the 1930s. Laubach decided to spend one year trying to live every waking minute in conscious listening to God. When he told friends he planned to do this, they said it was impossible. At first I had to agree with them. I live in an age in which many Christians don't even listen to God several times a day, let alone every minute.

Even if his plan were possible, was it excessive? How could he get anything else done? How could he avoid the endless distractions of work and conversation and entertainment and chores that fill up life? In one of the letters he wrote during his experiment, Laubach explained—

We can keep two things in mind at once. Indeed we cannot keep one thing in mind more than half a second. Mind is a flowing something. It oscillates. Concentration is merely the continuous return to the same problem from a million angles. Can I bring God back in my mind-flow every few seconds so that God shall always be in my mind as an after-image? I choose to make the rest of my life an experiment in answering this question.[1]

For Laubach, a man of service to others, part of filling his thoughts with God every minute included asking God what he should do for those around him and what he should say to them. Part of his resolve was to "be as wide open toward people and their need as I am toward God."[2] He knew people would criticize his experiment as too introspective. He decided to take the risk anyway. He knew he would not be able to live up to his plan for an entire year without fail, but he didn't let that fear of failure stop him.

Laubach also didn't recommend his approach for everyone. He told readers not to try it unless they felt dissatisfied with their own relationship with God. As for himself, he felt disgusted with the pettiness and inconsequentiality of much of his life. He was tired of small talk. He was tired of spiritual drift. He wanted a richer spiritual life.

For the most part, as he reports in a series of "letters" throughout the year, his plan worked. He started each morning by compelling his mind "to open straight out toward God. I wait and listen with determined sensitiveness. . . . I determine not to get out of bed until that mind-set, that concentration upon God, is settled." Focusing so intently on God did not slow him down in completing his daily tasks or serving those around him. He wrote, "The concentration on God is strenuous, but everything else has ceased to be so. I think more clearly, I forget less frequently. Things which I did with a strain before, I now do easily and with no effort whatever. I worry about nothing, and lose no sleep."[3]

Laubach found that his deeper awareness of God's presence caused him to treat people differently and also changed how people thought of him. Far from making him too introspective, his experiment actually took the focus *off* himself and allowed him to enjoy other people and the world around him more than before. Although most people around him were not aware of his experiment, they sensed a change in him and were more drawn to him. As he put it, "And I must witness that people outside are treating me differently. . . . People are becoming friendly who suspected or neglected me. I feel, I *feel* like one who has had his violin out of tune with the orchestra and at last is in harmony with the music of the universe."[4] He came to believe that it was important to saturate himself with God's presence on a "mount of trans-figuration" in order to shine brightly with God's light when he went to serve those who depended on him.

Laubach sometimes failed in his effort to stay close to God and was embarrassed when he lost his patience or snapped at someone, especially when that person was aware of his experiment and would wonder why he wasn't living up to it.

I've never tried turning my mind to God every minute the way Laubach did. I doubt I could sustain that kind of intensity for very long. Maybe for most Christians it's too much to expect. But what I love about what he did, and what I want to find a way to emulate, is that he threw open his entire life—every minute of his life—to God's presence and leading. I was hesitant to mention Laubach's experience as an example because it sounds so eccentric, but like him, I'm tired of a faith that so confines God to certain "sacred" spaces and leaves Him out of the vast majority of life.

This is not to say that living in relationship with God should mean thinking about Him every second, just as being in relationship with a person doesn't mean constant focus on that person. But a *sustained* neglect of God's presence is a quenching of the Spirit, just as sustained neglect of someone you love quenches that relationship. A *little* neglect of God's presence leads to even more. Distract me for a day, then a week, and I begin to confine God to a smaller and smaller place in my thoughts and actions. I spend less and less time praying, reading the Bible, and loving and serving others. I may give up some of those actions altogether. I promise to return to them "when things calm down," which never happens. Eventually I begin to think of God as someone nice I visit at church occasionally.

Is "Relationship" the Right Word to Describe How We Connect with God?

Many people become addicted to the mundane, or the concrete realities of life. Life becomes nothing more than a series of tasks and details—going to work, driving a car, buying a television set, squishing sand between their toes at the beach, eating a bowl of cereal, trying to remember to send that birthday card, ironing a shirt. Everybody lives much of life carrying out routine chores and enjoying ordinary experiences, of course, but it's easy to begin to believe that life is *nothing more than* those commonplace details.

Even Christians who ostensibly believe that reality transcends the everyday world around them—who believe that God has invaded their lives and that they are active members of the kingdom of God ushered in by Jesus Christ—can begin to live *as if* their concerns and interests and passions go no further than work and fun and movies and sports and cleaning out the garage and getting a better car someday. The key to waking up to the deeper realities of God's presence and our participation in His kingdom is not to set aside the mundane realities but rather to put them in their proper perspective, to see that they are not everything.

What do Christians mean when they speak of having a personal relationship with God? What did Laubach mean when he talked about listening to God? A relationship with God, just like a relationship with another person, has many facets. One way Christians know Him is to have a *direct* sense of His presence, often in times of worship or prayer. This way of knowing God is often filled with emotion as they feel God's loving Spirit right there with them, filling up the room.

But they may also know Him in less direct and emotional ways, such as when He speaks to them through Scripture. They may also sense His presence less directly by recognizing His influence in the things He created—in the beauty of mountains, oceans, animals, music, good food; and the joy of running and laughing and resting. They may also see His hand at work in circumstances, when a situation has worked out in such a manner that they believe had to be His influence.

What does it mean when Christians say God speaks to them? I believe God speaks in many ways. At times His presence comes as quiet, loving assurance to my soul. At other times it comes as conviction, the sense that what I am doing or thinking about doing is morally wrong and that I should step away from it. At times I experience Him in ways that provoke awe and wonder and love, a communion with Him that needs no words and that is embodied in the joy of simply being present with someone. At times, especially through Scripture and sermons and other teaching, His presence speaks guidance and instruction.

It's easy for skeptics to dismiss or mock the idea of God's presence in the lives of Christians. They reduce it to Christians hearing voices in their heads or other descriptions that overlook the complexity and mystery of how God really communicates. I have never heard God's audible voice, and I have talked to only a few Christians who say they have heard God audibly on a couple of miraculous occasions. That is hardly ever how the Holy Spirit works and is rarely what Christians claim. But I do sense God's leading in many ways.

These impressions of the Holy Spirit should be tested. Do my impressions align with Scripture, with what I know of God's character? Am I being honest with myself about my own thoughts and motivations? We "know in part," but if having a relationship with God means anything, it means interacting with Him in all the ways available to us—in prayer, in worship, in connection with the Body of Christ. As Dallas Willard puts it,

> The way of Jesus Christ is a way of *firsthand interaction*—knowing by acquaintance—direct awareness of him and his kingdom. Rarely will it involve anything like the sense perception of the Eternal provided to John and Thomas and the other apostles of Jesus. But you can't really sustain a kingdom life, a life "not of this world," without such interaction with the King.[5]

At times I am not consciously aware of God at all, even when I'm still in close relationship with Him. For example, when I'm in the classroom at my university, I get so absorbed in teaching that no other reality exists for me during that hour. If I'm teaching American literature, then the world of Faulkner or Dickinson or Frost, and the students' discussion of these writers, fills every corner of my mind. I sometimes get so lost in this reality that when the class time ends and I stop to give reminders for the next class, I can't remember what day it is. I have to stop a moment and reconnect myself to the mundane reality of the day of the week. I'm not consciously aware of my relationship with God in that hour, or with my wife or kids or friends, for that matter.

Later that evening, another reality might grip me as I attend my daughter's softball game. I enter into it casually, just another routine game in her schedule, but as the score gets close and my daughter goes up to bat with the potential of knocking in the winning run, all other reality except for this game ceases to exist. I so want her to hit that ball! I want the team to win. I stand up and cheer. A game that a couple hours earlier was nothing more than an obligation on my schedule now suddenly *matters* and obliterates everything else. At that point the literature that so absorbed me earlier is the farthest thing from my mind. Mark Twain and Robert Frost and William Faulkner never enter my thinking. Neither does my commitment to God.

Then the game is over, and even on the way home, my daughter's elation or disappointment fades, and she starts telling me her plans for the next day. Within a couple of days, we may barely remember that game at all.

When I'm caught in the grip of either of those slices of reality, softball or class, I give little thought to God or to any of the other Big Issues I mentioned earlier, such as death or heaven. But the fact that I don't pray to God about anything other than softball during a softball game doesn't mean I'm not a committed Christian any more than not thinking about my wife during my American literature class means I'm not a faithful husband.

In a sense I live in denial of my wife during class, but later in that day I call her. Later that afternoon I go home to her. We talk, we have dinner, we take the kids somewhere. We're connected again. Now if I didn't come home that night, the next night, or the next without explanation, that would soon become a problem. If I decided to spend only one hour with her a week, our marriage would fray. If I stopped doing even that and basically ignored her altogether, divorce would loom. That kind of neglect would be a quenching of the marriage. The relationship could not survive it.

Many Christians do something similar in their relationship with God. The problem is not that other slices of reality sometimes push awareness of Him into the background. That is naturally going to happen. The problem comes when those other slices of reality push Him into a smaller and smaller space—until He has no place whatsoever. At that point faith can die, and the person may begin to wonder whether he or she ever knew Him at all and whether a relationship with Him is even possible or desirable. The person never *decided* to end the relationship, but it died anyway.

Why Did Jesus Keep Sneaking Away?

Jesus spent much of His earthly ministry sneaking away from the crowds and responsibilities and expectations of others so that He could be alone to pray to the Father. You can't even get through the first chapter of Mark before the Gospel writer tells about Jesus taking off without telling anybody so He can find somewhere to pray.

That chapter tells about a particular day when Jesus went to a city where everybody in town crowded in at the door as He healed one person after another. He was immensely popular in that town. He was helping people. He was fulfilling His mission. Still, for Jesus it was not complete unless He stayed close to the Father.

It wasn't easy escaping the crowds and the disciples and the tug of everyone's requests. He had to slip out early in the morning—"while it was still dark," the chapter says—to find a "desolate place" where He could pray. The disciples went out searching for Him, and when they found Him they said, "Everyone is looking for you." The verse doesn't tell what tone of voice they used, but it sounds like a complaint to me. Do their words carry the sense of "Everybody's looking for you, so why on earth are you hiding out here alone in the middle of nowhere?"

Jesus knew better. He knew the deceptive lure of anything—even good works—that might pull Him away from the Father. He healed. He preached. He spent time connecting with the Father. If even Jesus needed to go out of His way to make sure He spent time alone in prayer, then what about the rest of us?

Jesus' behavior shows two things. One is that it is possible to stay awake to God's presence even in the midst of a chaotic life. The second is that staying awake to God's presence doesn't happen automatically. Jesus woke up early in the morning, while it was still dark (in a world without electric lights or coffee makers, a world in which dark meant *dark*) in order to flee to the desolate spot to pray. He knew that you can't put your spiritual life on automatic pilot and expect it to thrive.

Being spiritually awake is not our default position. Our default position is drift, spiritual sleep, and a gradual eroding of faith. When I see Jesus praying in this scene and others, including in His agonizing night at Gethsemane, He teaches me the most important lesson I've ever learned about prayer: you have to fling yourself at it. No matter what else is vying for your energy and attention, you have to set it all aside, push yourself into the darkness if you have to, and go to the place of prayer—you and the Father staying in close connection. That's what Jesus did. That's what I want to do.

Is It Possible Anymore to Stay Focused on *Anything*?

The world we live in is not making it any easier to wake up to God's presence. The modern society is set up to *scatter* our focus more than ever. In many ways previous generations could concentrate more intently—on God or anything else—because they had much less fighting for their attention. I have taught journalism courses in which I show students newspapers from the 1800s that featured small print, long blocks of unbroken type extending all the way down the page, and cramped columns with hardly any space in between. The students wonder how readers could possibly have put up with such an uncomfortable layout. I demonstrate how to read such a newspaper. You hold it closer to your face than any of us are accustomed to and look closely at each line as you read carefully down the page, using your finger as a guide. You take in each sentence. You *read*. You concentrate.

That's not how we consume news today. Instead, we skip around from story to story, glancing at a headline here, a paragraph or two there, a photo caption, back to another headline. In the unlikely event that we're actually reading the news on *paper*, we flip through the pages, stopping only on the things that grab our attention. Hardly anyone reads the whole paper from top to bottom, start to finish. Those who get their news on the Internet develop even shorter attention spans, flipping from web site to web site, scanning the headlines, popping into a story here and there, watching a minute or two of video, skipping to the next story. Our attention is further scattered with thousands of Facebook posts, Twitter messages, blogs, television programs, text messages, radio broadcasts, movies, and books.

Every day our concentration is pulled in a thousand different directions. Jesus, even in the days before all this frenetic technology had been invented, had to escape to a desolate place to practice the kind of focused prayer He considered essential. Where could He have gone to escape the noise in *our* culture? Where is the desolate place where we can go for deep prayer and communion with God today? How many of us even try to find it?

We live in a culture in which it is not only more difficult than ever before to concentrate deeply on God but in which it is harder to concentrate on *anything*. A recent Kaiser Family Foundation study reported that children ages eight to eighteen spend an average of seven hours and thirty-eight minutes a day on entertainment media. Often they are accessing more than one media source at a time, such as texting while watching television and listening to music, so if you add up the time spent in all those streams, the total is nearly eleven hours a day.[6]

How fragmented is our thinking? Another recent study showed that teens ages thirteen to seventeen send and receive an average of 3,339 text messages a month. Adults have not yet reached that enormous average, although the numbers are steadily climbing.[7]

I have described the modern condition as spiritual "sleep," but it certainly doesn't *feel* like sleep when we're experiencing it—just the opposite. It's energizing to have those messages flying and those Internet pages popping up with photos and videos and updates and sparkling ideas to think about for a few minutes before jumping to the next one. Jesus must have felt the same satisfying buzz from the crowds and the attention and the gratitude of the people He healed and the families who brought them. Stepping away from that to pray alone in the dark at the desolate place may have taken a courageous act of will, but Jesus knew it was necessary for His own spiritual health.

I follow a discipline of not accessing e-mail or the Internet until after my morning time of writing and prayer and Scripture reading. By the time I finally connect, I fcel a surge of excitement, even relief, to finally be able to re-enter the electronic flow of messages and information. It's like the jolt of a strong cup of coffee. I certainly wouldn't want to give it up. It's good to be connected to friends, to conduct business, to be plugged into the world around me. But I also know that I don't want to give up what happens *before* I hit that button to connect in those early morning hours as I let God's Word flow over me and as I pray and direct my mind toward Him.

I also do my most concentrated writing in those pre-connected hours, before the buzz of the day splinters my focus. If something prevents me from having that time, or if I give in to the temptation to connect to the online buzz early, it affects my entire day. I may never get another opportunity that day to pray deeply to God or to push my thoughts toward Him in a way that will align everything I do more closely to my relationship with Him and with my work as a citizen of His kingdom.

Waking Up

Before I can wake up to God's presence, I first have to battle the big part of me that simply doesn't care that much about the spiritual side of life. When directly confronted, I say, "Of course I care. My relationship with Jesus Christ is the most important thing in my life." That is true. Most of the time, however, I am *not* directly confronted. Most of the time nobody knows or cares where I stand spiritually. I'm left to follow Christ passionately or else drift along casually as I see fit. While part of me wants to be more like Frank Laubach or other spiritual giants I know and follow God with greater intensity, a big part of me also wants to simply float along. I don't want to direct my attention toward something. I want to let it drift wherever it feels like going.

Let's face it—the spiritual life can seem a little dull, especially if we buy into the stereotypes about it. Instead of picturing it as being embodied by someone enjoying a soul-shaking, joyful, life-embracing relationship with God, people might picture the cliché of a too-pious, overly religious, life-denying person spouting rote prayers in a sterile room. Many get stuck in that cliché and never taste the joy of God's presence. They don't even think they would want to.

I believe the enemy of our soul doesn't have to make us believe that God doesn't exist or that Christian theology is false in order to defeat us. It's enough simply to turn God into a boring abstraction to whom we feel we should pay homage occasionally but who really doesn't have much to do with real life. We treat Him with the respect we might give to an ancient aunt we visit at her retirement home, even though we barely knew her in the first place.

How do we *see* God for who He really is? How do we wake up to the joy that a closer relationship with Him could bring? I believe God has scattered messages to us throughout the world. We miss most of them. His message is in the face of the hurting person who needs our help. His Spirit is in the soaring melody of a song, in the crash of an ocean wave, in the intricacy of the careful work of the intellect, in the spiritual surge of a revival. The purpose of the rest of this book is to help awaken you to these life-giving messages. If God has chosen to show up right here where I live, I don't want to miss Him.

Go to beaconhillbooks.com for a free downloadable study guide that includes questions for deeper personal reflection as well as activities for use in a small-group setting.

four ☒ ☒ ☒
GOD IN THE ORDINARY
Encountering Him in the World He Created

■ For many years my father lovingly restored a black '51 Chevy. I remember how surprised I was the day he bought it. I looked out in the driveway, and there it was, dirty and weather-beaten from having sat for years outside an Indiana farmhouse. Over the next few years Dad took his time repairing and repainting the car inside and out until it gleamed. He took it to some car shows, but only if there was no threat of rain. For over ten years not a drop of rain fell on it.

To see that car was immediately to think of my dad. He sold it several years ago, but to this day, if I see a car that looks anything like it, I immediately think of him. If I see a picture of it, thoughts of Dad flood my mind. When I wrote a novel several years ago with a character loosely based on my father, I made that car a central symbol.

Some people are so closely connected to certain places or objects that encountering those things makes them feel almost as if they are in their presence. When my kids are away on a camping trip, I can walk into their bedrooms and feel close to them as I glance at their posters and toys and books. I can't enter a Starbucks without thinking of my wife, with whom I've spent many good hours there. Certain gifts I have received over the years immediately bring to mind the faces of the friends who gave them to me.

In the same way, when I spend time in nature, away from my ordinary routine, I sense God's presence. From my house it takes a little less than an hour to make my way through belligerent southern California freeway traffic to get to Laguna Beach, my favorite beach in our area. I've been there countless times, but it's impossible for me not to sense God's power and presence as I walk along that shore and feel the sun and sand hit my face and hear the rhythmical swoosh of waves surging in. The glints of light across the vast ocean are like no other sight in the world. I could walk or sit for hours—and sometimes do—and listen to seagulls and wind and water and laughter of children.

At the north end of the beach, up a hill, is the most beautiful cliff-side walk I have ever been on. Any single element of this walk would make the whole trip worth it—the dramatic steep drop of cliffs, the panoramic view of the ocean, the rocky beaches at the bottom of the cliff, the mountains behind us, the warm sunshine, the trees and flowers along the sidewalks and down the hillsides, the ocean breeze.

Whenever my wife and I take this walk, we see people all around us taking photographs. Sometimes they ask us to take a photo for them so they can insert themselves into the scene. They can't get enough of it. Who can blame them? God's fingerprints are all over this place. It's as if He is saying, *Look at what I can do. See this little glimpse? This is only the beginning.*

We sometimes walk and sit along this stretch all afternoon and evening, waiting for the sunset. Everything inside

GOD IN THE ORDINARY

me slows down in this place, and I sense God's presence. I can no more shut Him out of my mind when I'm here than I can keep my dad out of my mind when I come across a 1951 Chevy. A scene of nature like this not only reminds people of God but also invites them toward Him. They want to *interact* with His handiwork and find Him in it. They want not only to look at the ocean—they also want to jump into those waves. They want to climb those mountains. They want to hike the trails. They want to ride boats across the water. They want to celebrate this creation. The writer of Psalm 104 tries to capture the intertwining of God's presence with nature when he says,

He wraps himself in light as with a garment;
he stretches out the heavens like a tent
and lays the beams of his upper chambers on their
waters.
He makes the clouds his chariot and rides on the wings
of the wind.
He makes winds his messengers, flames of fire his servants (*Psalm 104:2-4*).

The psalmist goes on to celebrate mountains, valleys, birds, beasts, wine, oil, sun, moon, and all living creatures:

When you send your Spirit,
they are created,
and you renew the face of the earth. May the glory of
the Lord endure forever;
May the LORD rejoice in his works.
He looks at the earth, and it trembles; he touches the
mountains, and they smoke.
I will sing to the LORD all my life;
I will sing praise to my God as long as I live (*Psalm
104:30-33*).

45

I know just how he feels. I also think God should celebrate His creation, and I believe I sometimes sense Him doing that with me as I take time to go out and enjoy the incredible world He has made.

Many people sense God in nature before they know Him in any other way. While researching *God in Pursuit*, I was captivated by the conversion story of diplomat and congresswoman Clare Booth Luce, who includes in her story an experience on the beach as a teenager that was so profound and unexpected that she had no categories in her thinking to define it. She forgot about this incident for years, but it brought her tremendous joy when it came back to her many months after her Christian conversion. She realized it played a part in her conversion, at least subconsciously, but she couldn't describe exactly how.

When she was about sixteen years old, she stood alone on the beach for a long time in the early morning. She felt a distinct sense of solitariness. It was a radiant day. Then something happened:

I expect that the easiest thing is to say that suddenly SOMETHING WAS. My whole soul was cleft clean by it, as a silk veil slit by a shining sword. And I *knew*. I do not now know what I knew. I remember that I didn't know even then. That is, I didn't *know* with any "faculty." It was not in my mind or heart or bloodstream. But whatever it was I knew; it was something that made ENORMOUS SENSE. . . . Then joy abounded in all of me. Or rather, I abounded in joy.[1]

A Christian reading that description might immediately recognize the presence of the Holy Spirit in that scene. In a foreshadowing of her conversion, God was drawing her toward Him. It took years for her to make sense of this incident for herself. Many people have similar spiritual encounters with nature but don't know what to do with them. Often they remain vague, inspiring moments that fade away. But as with music, another force that like nature is imbued with God's presence, these encounters can be stepping stones toward a more fully realized relationship with God.

Why Did God Bother to Make His Creation Beautiful?

A couple years ago I read a variety of books by scientists on the controversies of religion, the existence of God, creation, evolution, and related issues. I chose books by writers at various points on the spectrum of belief, from atheists to Christians. Most of the writers, whether Christian or not, did not rely on the beauty or inspiration of nature, or God's presence in it, to construct their arguments. That didn't surprise me. They work in a different realm with different tools. They discuss theories and numbers and laws of physics. One writer whose book I enjoyed was Karl Giberson, a scientist, Christian, and professor of physics at Eastern Nazarene College.

After taking the reader through a careful analysis of various views and approaches toward evolution and related ideas from a scientific point of view, Giberson surprised me in his last chapter by describing the beauty and serenity of the isolated lake where he has taken a vacation every summer since his childhood. He loves to watch the beavers and birds and listen to the whisper of leaves and cascading of water. He writes, "Although I am a scientist and a great enthusiast for that approach to understanding the world, I often find myself thinking that our scientific understanding is an inadequate abstraction, that only a portion of reality has been captured in its nets. And maybe that portion is smaller than we think."[2]

Science, Giberson points out, likes to use the language and metaphors of engineering and math. "We tend to view the eye as an optical device, the brain as computational, and the knee as mechanical," he says. But phenomena "without engineering analogs, like our sense of humor or great enthusiasm to play in rock bands, seems harder to understand."[3] Why is nature so beautiful? Why does it thrill and inspire? From a strictly scientific or "mechanical" standpoint, there is no need for it to be so pleasing, so artistic and aesthetically diverse.

Maybe the answer is that nature exists for more than simply a functional purpose. Maybe God is using it, as He uses music—another unnecessarily beautiful force from any functional point of view—to express himself. Maybe He is using it to reach us. Maybe He watches us, pleased, as we experience it with awe. Maybe He puts it there to point the way to Him.

This is not to say that nature is a Garden of Eden. It isn't. The world, nature and humans included, is fallen, and every aspect of creation is affected by that fallen state. Romans 8:22 says that "the whole creation has been groaning as in the pains of childbirth right up to the present time." Fallen nature includes not only beauty but also cruelty, destruction, illness, decay, and death. In spite of its harshness, however, nature as a whole is still so imbued with the artistic presence of its Creator that it's hard to be in it very long without being reminded of Him.

The Universe as a Key to God's Extravagance

I love astronomy. I'm attracted by the huge numbers involved—the vast distances, the monster stars, the extreme temperatures, the black holes, the earth-sized storms on planets devoid of life. I know that people with a worldview of scientific naturalism believe God had nothing to do with the creation of all these exotic worlds. They believe they sprang up on their own through natural processes.

But that is not my worldview. I believe God created it all through whatever natural processes He may have chosen. Some contemplate the vastness and complexity of the universe and move farther away from God. I see the same jewels of His creation and feel closer to Him. *Why, I wonder, did He create all these things? What is His purpose in allowing human beings to discover them? What may He do with all of it in eternity?*

I regularly come across news stories about astronomy that blow me away. I save them and keep reading them, stunned at their implications. I read, for instance, about a new sun, a "monster star," that has been discovered, that makes our own sun seem tiny by comparison. I have read a little about our own sun, and I know it is so massive and bright and hot that it isn't easy to outshine it. Our own sun is so huge that a million earths would fit inside it. I learned from Curt Suplee of *National Geographic* magazine that inside our own sun "the solar core is so dense that a single photon, the fundamental unit of light, can't go even a fraction of a millimeter before banging into some subatomic particle, where it is scattered or absorbed and re-emitted. As a result, it can take hundreds of thousands of years for a photon to ricochet its way nearly half a million miles to the sun's surface." Our sun is so bright that it is too powerful for me to look at directly, even though it is ninety-three million miles away.[4] And yet they have found a monster star that makes this sun look tiny by comparison? How big is it?

The little news article that I read online—an article casually tucked into a list of articles about celebrity scandals, economic forecasts, and political wrangling—states that this newly discovered star is *ten million times brighter* than our sun. Think about that. Look out your window and see the bright sunshine whose source is too dangerous for you to gaze at directly, and imagine something ten million times brighter. I can hardly fathom something twice as bright, or ten times as bright. But *ten million* times brighter? It also has a mass that is two hundred sixty-five times more than our sun. It's more than one hundred sixty-five thousand light years away from the Milky Way galaxy.[5] One light year, by the way, is about six trillion miles.

God's *extravagance* in creating such a universe astonishes me. Why did He put that sun there, so unfathomably big and bright, so incomprehensibly far away? Between earth and that star, as far as we know, not a single human being or any other living creature has ever existed. All that space and stars and planets without life, without consciousness, without anyone to make use of those planets or appreciate them. Why?

Why did He create me and place me on this masterpiece of a planet, a place so tiny in comparison with the rest of His creation and yet so crammed with life? My consciousness is a miracle in itself, as impressive as a massive sun of whatever brightness. The planet I get to walk is a playground of a place in comparison to the rest of the universe. I play baseball with my children and listen to music and swim in the ocean and jog along the foothills and teach literature at my university and worship in a church and imagine and pray and laugh in this place that my fellow humans and I share with countless birds and whales and goldfish and dogs and lizards and tarantulas and sagebrush and dandelions and lemon trees and endless other treasures I could put on this list. The mystery of all this pushes me toward God.

If I dwell on the enormity of the universe, I lean toward one of two responses. One possibility is despair that I am so small and insignificant. I am a tiny speck in a huge expanse of matter. I also have a very short shelf life. Almost every day I glance through a series of favorite web sites, and one that humbles me most is the *National Geographic* site. I could list many pages of articles from that site that remind me of my relative insignificance with creation, but one recent one that's typical is an article that tells of the discovery of the most massive and distant cloud of water ever found in the universe. Here is the first sentence: "Weighing in at forty billion times the mass of earth, the giant cloud of mist swaddles a type of actively feeding supermassive black hole known as a quasar."[6] Maybe some people can skim over a sentence like that as casually as if they were reading the previous day's sports scores, but I get stuck there and have to give my imagination some time to try to digest such an amazing fact.

A few paragraphs later I learn that the water around this quasar is enough to fill all the oceans on earth more than 140 trillion times. The rest of the article is a blur. I can't take it in. When people want to use a metaphor to describe something as small, they sometimes say the thing is "like a drop in the ocean." But if you took *all* the oceans of earth and poured them into this water cloud, they would not even add up to a comparative drop. And did I mention that this water is in a galaxy twelve billion light-years away? And did I mention that elsewhere on the *National Geographic* web site in a section giving basic astronomical facts, I am informed that the entire galaxy in which this water resides doesn't even amount to a drop in the ocean of all the other galaxies: "The number of galaxies cannot be counted—the observable universe alone may contain 100 billion."[7]

Reading *National Geographic* is dangerous for me. I read it only when I have some time to let my brain wander through the cloud of wonder that these facts create. And while one response that I'm tempted to take toward my tininess in the scheme of things is resignation or despair, as a Christian I choose a different response. I push myself toward God and rely on His love alone to give significance to my life. Apart from Him, I am no more important than a rock on a lifeless planet in an unnamed galaxy trillions of lightyears away. But if the Creator of all of this loves me, which all the evidence of His presence and words of Scripture and the testimony of my fellow believers now and across time indicate, then I am truly valuable indeed. I am so small that there is nothing I can do to earn significance in such a universe. My puny attempts would be laughable, but God's valuing of me confers value. I am His child. Romans 8 calls me an heir to this staggering creation, a co-heir with Christ. God has given me and my brothers and sisters this universe as a playground for eternity. We might as well start playing.

Accepting this inheritance in the posture of a grateful child is the only attitude that makes sense in a universe in which we are so tiny. When Jesus' disciples asked Him who is the greatest in the kingdom of heaven, He answered, "Truly I tell you, unless you change and become like little children, you will never enter the kingdom of heaven. Therefore, whoever takes the lowly position of this child is the greatest in the kingdom of heaven" (Matthew 18:3-4).

No wonder Jesus lived and taught the way He did. No one else had such a complete understanding of the cosmos and our place in it. He was there for the creation of the billions of galaxies. He knew the smallness and temporariness of earthly possessions and achievements. He spent no time gathering wealth or courting fame. He told us not to bother with it either. "Do not store up for yourselves treasures on earth, where moths and rust destroy, and where thieves break in and steal," he said. "But store up for yourselves treasures in heaven, where moths and vermin do not destroy, and where thieves do not break in and steal" (Matthew 6:19-20). We'll inherit all of it eventually. In the meantime, we can rest in the liberation of being a beloved child.

From the Top of the Hill the World Looks Different

I don't need to contemplate galaxies billions of light-years away in order to let nature shift my perspective and draw me closer to God. That change of outlook can happen in the natural world much closer to home.

I live in the foothills of southern California, and in no more than a forty-minute hike from my house, I can be high enough in the hills that I can see several towns, freeways, and the distant buildings of downtown Los Angeles spread out before me.

From the top of the hill on my favorite hiking path, I can pick out my own house as a speck in the middle of a neighborhood below. From that height my house looks so small and is so obscured by trees that I have trouble finding it, even though I have seen it from up there many times. What a contrast from when I'm down there *inside* my house, and it feels so big! The house feels big not because of its square footage, which is pretty modest, but because the house is its own little universe stuffed with work and stress and dreams and meals and conversations and love and frustration. From the top of the foothills trail just minutes away, it is one of hundreds of houses within my view, barely significant. If it were wiped from the landscape, no one from up there would even notice.

When I'm toiling away inside my little house, I can easily fall into the illusion that I control my life. This is my domain, and if I simply make the right decisions and take the right actions, I can make things turn out the way I want them to. I give allegiance to God, but I'm the one bending reality to my will. I don't state it that directly. I wouldn't admit to believing it. But I often live as if my house were a little spaceship floating through the universe, and I am the captain.

Gazing down from the mountain strips me of that illusion of control. From up there I can barely even *find* my house, let alone steer its course or determine its fate. I'm not really controlling any of it. Someone far bigger is in control. I am a resident, a soldier maybe, but not the captain. I see that more clearly from up there. If I want to find who is in control, I have to look far outside myself, to Someone big enough to encompass the vastness.

It's quiet at the top of that mountain. Everything slows down up there. There is a stillness in the trees and grass and plants of those hills that is not so easy to find in the human-made atmosphere below. I find that serenity not only in these foothills but also in almost any part of nature that I turn to. It's there on the beach as the waves surge in with their calming rhythm. It's there on the forest trail as I stand and look up at the massive trees that are thriving and growing but also still and unhurried, the wind in the leaves and call of birds offering a soothing soundtrack.

I don't know of any era in history when there was a greater need for deliberately setting aside time to encounter God in nature than in our own frantic age. For some, such times may even be necessary for spiritual survival. Whether your time in nature is a quiet walk on a trail near your home or a spiritual retreat in a distant cabin or a ski trip in the mountains, nature can be a place where we can more readily penetrate that veil that separates us from God's presence. Because He created and inhabits the natural world, it may be easier to sense Him there. The awe-inspiring beauty may bring Him to mind, and the solitude may create the atmosphere of openness toward His Spirit—but only if you allow it to happen. A serene atmosphere doesn't automatically bring people close to God—it merely makes it easier for them to find Him.

It's certainly possible to spend time in nature without ever giving God a thought. It's also possible to think of nature as nothing more than a pastime for select groups of people—mountain climbers and bird-watchers and fishermen. But I believe God created it for all of us and that He invites us to go to it as often as we can. When Jesus needed to pray, He didn't go farther into the cities and villages, with all the crowds and noise. He slipped off to an isolated spot where He could hear the Father better. I need to learn to run off the way Jesus did. I can see the foothills from my window, and the trail is only minutes away, but I usually say I'm too busy to take that hike. The pull of everyday demands is usually greater than the more subtle promise of my experience at the top of the favorite hill. I need to learn to build that hike into my schedule, or be more willing to drop everything occasionally and go.

Where Were You When God Created the Wonders of the Universe?

Throughout the excruciating ordeal of Job in the Bible, one of his greatest frustrations is God's *silence* in the midst of suffering. When God finally breaks that silence near the end of the book, He doesn't talk about suffering. Instead, He asks Job about a very different topic—nature. God asks,

"Where were you when I laid the earth's foundation? Tell me, if you understand. Who marked off its dimensions? Surely you know! Who stretched a measuring line across it? On what were its footings set, or who laid its cornerstone—while the morning stars sang together and all the angels shouted for joy?" (Job 38:4-7).

Those rhetorical questions alone would have been tough for Job to deal with, but God doesn't stop there. He not only puts Job on the spot about the creation of the world, but He also continues to bombard him with questions about the other wonders of the universe. How much did Job have to do with separating the land from the sea or creating morning? Has he ever walked in the recesses of the deep, or has he seen the gates of death? Where does light come from? How about darkness? Can Job make it rain or snow? Can he cause ice or frost to form? How about stars and planets? Can he bring those into being?

And what about the animal world? God asks, "Do you give the horse his strength or clothe his neck with a flowing mane? Do you make it leap like a locust, striking terror with his proud snorting?" (Job 39:19-20). What about mountain goats and donkeys and hawks and eagles? Does Job control them or even understand them? On and on goes this remarkable poetic litany, and Job is appropriately overwhelmed.

When he gets a chance to answer God, he has to admit that he has no reply. "I put my hand over my mouth," he says, and repents of trying to speak about "things too wonderful for me to know" (Job 40:4; 42:3).

These chapters are worth reading as a reminder of how little any of us know or control, even in a technologically advanced era. To move toward God is to move away from the illusion of self-sufficiency. God's questions to Job are another way of saying what Jesus told His disciples: that the only way to enter the kingdom of heaven is to approach it like a child. Certainly it is not an anti-intellectual message. The message is not "You can't know everything, so don't even try to understand the universe." The message is "The mystery of the universe is beyond your limits. But don't despair. God loves you. You are His child. In the midst of what is beyond your comprehension, trust Him."

When I was on a business trip away from my family recently, my wife told me on the phone that it wasn't as hard as it used to be to watch the kids alone. "They're more self-sufficient now," she said. We both knew what she meant, but self-sufficient? Then why don't they pay the mortgage? Or the water bill? Why do we still have to shoo them off to school and take them to sports practices and haul in piles of groceries for them each week?

They're not really self-sufficient. They can entertain themselves now, dress themselves, feed themselves, do their homework, play musical instruments, and perform feats on the athletic field that we would have thought miraculous for them a few years ago. They also *think* they don't need us much. Often as parents we are merely background details to them now, people to facilitate their activities.

That's how many people think of God. He may exist, but He's in the background, not really someone to worry much about. We're self-sufficient. We don't need Him. But who gave us the air to breathe, the earth to live on, the water to drink, the beauty to savor, the other humans to love?

Though often my kids think they don't need me, something always brings them back—maybe my absence for a few days, a crisis, or a sudden burst of love. Then they *see* me again, and I get the unexpected hug or loving word.

The natural world can act in a similar way to wake me up toward God. I may not think much about Him much for a while, but then a waterfall or sunset or summer breeze wakes me up, and I run to Him in gratitude. Whether I stand at the top of the mountain trail overlooking my house, on the beach looking out on the sea, or in the shade of the trees in my own backyard playing kickball with my kids, I want to learn to open my arms in thankfulness more often for the privilege I enjoy as God's child to play in His creation.

Go to beaconhillbooks.com for a free downloadable study guide that includes questions for deeper personal reflection as well as activities for use in a small-group setting.

five ☒ ☒ ☒
GOD IN THE ORDINARY
He Disguises Himself in People

■ Of all my physical abilities, the one I would most dread losing is my sight. I love to read, I love to see my family and friends, I love to be able to drive, I love all the richness of experience that sight affords. I know blind people compensate and cope, but I have long thought that blindness would be one of the hardest conditions to bear.

One of my favorite chapters in Annie Dillard's outstanding book *Pilgrim at Tinker Creek* is called "Seeing." In it she tells of people who have been blind from birth but who gain their sight after surgery. I would have imagined that these newly sighted people would be thrilled with the way this new sense opens up the world to them, but their reactions are often much more complicated. One problem is that the patients who have just received sight don't know *what* they're seeing. They don't yet have a sense of depth perception or other spatial proportions that would help them make sense of what they're looking at. One doctor said of his newly sighted patient, "I have found in her no notion of size, for example, not even within the narrow limits which she might have encompassed with the aid of touch. Thus, when I asked her to show me how big her mother was, she did not stretch out her hands but set her two index fingers a few inches apart."[1] For many of these patients, the world is a "dazzle of color-patches" rather than a place of discernible objects and depths.

Not only do the newly sighted have trouble knowing what they are seeing, but these sights are so different from anything they have known before that they sometimes don't *want* to see them. Sight is too disruptive and disturbing. Dillard writes, "It oppresses them to realize, if they ever do at all, the tremendous size of the world, which they had previously conceived of as something touchingly manageable. It oppresses them to realize that they have been visible to people all along, perhaps unattractively so, without their knowledge or consent."[2] Some refuse to use their new sight, walking around with their eyes closed instead. One boy threatens to tear his eyes out if things don't go back to the way they were.

Others welcome sight with a sense of awe and astonishment. They stare with wonder at the simplest objects, a bunch of grapes or a tree with sunlight streaming through. One girl keeps her eyes shut for two weeks because she is overwhelmed by the world's brightness, but then she opens her eyes, and as she looks at each new thing, she keeps repeating, "Oh, God—how beautiful!"[3]

The responses of those who *see* the world for the first time are similar to how different people respond to experiencing the presence of God. For those who have been blind to Him for a long time, being confronted with that bright light of His presence may feel disorienting and even scary. They may prefer to keep their eyes tightly shut against Him in order not to have to come to terms with Him. Even if they do open their eyes to Him, they may not understand what they're seeing at first. They may see a blizzard of bright patches that don't make much sense. The intensity or confusion may cause them to close their eyes again and cling to the darker but more comprehensible world that felt safer. On the other hand, if they keep their eyes open, if they learn not only to see Him but also to *perceive* Him, then the fear may be gradually replaced by awe and love and gratitude. Like the girl who finally risked opening her eyes to the world's brightness, they can say of His presence, "Oh, God—how beautiful!"

Some people walk through the world and don't perceive God in it at all. I try to imagine what the world would look like if God's presence left physical clues wherever He went. What if I could see a purple stain wherever God had been? The church sanctuary where I worship would be covered in purple since I have perceived His Spirit so powerfully there. Every edition of the Bible would be a purple-letter edition. He made human beings in His image, so maybe His purple fingerprints would be all over the people around me. Music would produce not only sound but also a beautiful purple haze that would fill the air. The mountains, the trees—all of nature, God's creation—would be covered in purple. He created it all, so I guess there would be purple all over the place, with maybe some blank spots of evil. In other words, it would look pretty much like the world around me right now—except more purple! And yet it's so easy to walk through that world each day and not see Him.

When Jesus Doesn't Look the Way We Thought He Would

One reason people sometimes miss God's presence is that He comes disguised. People expect Him to show up one way, but instead He enters their lives in ways they weren't prepared for, in places and in people and at times they never anticipated. This has always been the case. Even when Jesus was in His most visible and recognizable form as He walked on earth, people still didn't recognize Him. The Jewish leaders and Roman officials who killed Him obviously missed the significance of who He was, but even His closest friends sometimes had trouble recognizing Him when He showed up in ways they didn't expect and had trouble accepting.

To me, the strangest examples of this are when Jesus appeared to His disciples after His resurrection. One of the surprising things about these appearances is how quiet they were. If there were ever a time for trumpet blasts and a booming voice from heaven and flashes of light across the sky, surely the resurrection—the rising from the dead after three days of Jesus Christ himself—would be cause for that kind of fanfare. But Jesus kept showing up in ways that were so understated that His own followers didn't even realize it was Him at first.

On the road to Emmaus Jesus walked along having an entire conversation with two men without their ever realizing who He was. They didn't realize it was Him until just seconds before He vanished out of their sight. He appeared to His disciples at another point, and they feared He was a spirit. Thomas didn't fully believe it was Jesus until He was given the opportunity to touch Jesus' hands and side.

And then there was the time when the resurrected Jesus showed up to have breakfast with Peter and some of the other disciples after they had spent a long and unsuccessful night fishing. At daybreak, as John 21 records it, while the men were still out in the boat, Jesus showed up on the shore and watched them. He was not announced by angel choirs or an earthquake. He just stood there, looking out at them. They didn't notice him. Finally He asked, "Children, do you have any fish?"

They didn't, so He helped them out a little. He didn't dispense spiritual advice or give the answers to life's deepest mysteries. Instead, He helped them with what they were doing right then—fishing, making a living, getting through the day.

"Cast the net on the right side of the boat, and you'll find some fish," He said. When they followed His advice and caught so many fish that they were unable to haul in the net, they finally recognized Him. When they came ashore and finally dragged in their net full of fish, Jesus continued to keep the encounter simple and low-key. He invited them to join Him for a breakfast of fish and bread. They caught one hundred fifty-three fish, but the net didn't tear.

Doesn't it seem strange that Scripture records the exact count of the fish? There are about a million things in the Bible I would love more details on—how tall was Jesus? What did He look like? What did His voice sound like? How often did He laugh? We don't get any of that, but from these fishermen we know exactly how many fish Jesus helped them catch. They were having breakfast with the resurrected Son of God, but somebody must have been over on the side counting. This is a fishing story. Jesus entered *their* daily lives. He cared about what mattered to them. A significant spiritual conversation follows, but first it's fish and breakfast and reminiscing.

Jesus entered into the ordinary details of life, as He still does today. He is just as close to you when you're sitting in traffic or shopping at the mall or getting chewed out by your boss as He is when you're staring at a stained-glass church window and listening to hymns. Will you recognize Him?

This fishing breakfast scene is not how I would have expected Jesus Christ to show up in triumph of His resurrection. It's no wonder they didn't recognize Him at first. Jesus warned us that we wouldn't always recognize Him when He comes. In Matthew 25:35-36, when Jesus is describing the final judgment, He says to His true followers, "I was hungry and you gave me something to eat, I was thirsty and you gave me something to drink. I was a stranger and you invited me in, I needed clothes and you clothed me, I was sick and you looked after me, I was in prison and you came to visit me." And what will they say to this? Really? We did all those things? For you? You were there? We missed those clues. When did we see you?

We all know His answer: "Whatever you did for one of the least of these brothers and sisters of mine, you did for me" (verse 40). Who are these "least of" people? Jesus gives them a few examples: hungry people, poor people, strangers, criminals. It's not hard to find the people Jesus was talking about. They are all around us. Maybe you fit in one or more of those groups yourself. It's not hard to find ways to give food and drink and clothing and love to the people Jesus referred to. Ministries to the poor and homeless and imprisoned abound. All you need is the *willingness* to serve and to give. The need is enormous. According to Richard Stearns, president of World Vision US, about 854 million people in the world do not have enough food to sustain them. Around 400 million children are hungry, and about 25,000 people a day—or about nine million a year—die of hunger.[4] Does thinking of those hungry people as Jesus make you more willing to help them?

The people Jesus was talking about are often people who *need* you in some way but don't necessarily have much to offer you in return. They're people right in front of you—but not necessarily the people you like the most or want to impress.

I squirm when I read what Jesus says in that passage. I wish He had worded it differently. If He had said, "I want you to love these people because it would show you're a good follower of mine," that would have been a little easier to take. I want to be a good follower. But He said, "When you did it to them, you did it to me." He equates himself with them. How I treat them is how I treat Him. And I wonder, was His list of the "least of these" people comprehensive, or might it also include others in my life who need but don't give? How about the ones who gripe and complain and whine and give me a hard time? How about the ones who call me names and blame me? How about those who made their own messes and then come to me for help to get out of it? Is Jesus saying, "I'm in those people. When you help those people, you help me. If you want me to show up, that's what I'll look like, strange as it may sound."

I don't want that to be true. If I'm honest about it, I don't even want to be in the same room with some of those people. To love them, I have to get outside of myself too much. I have to force myself out of the attitudes of distance I have built up against them, attitudes I feel justified in having developed. I have to walk up to them and treat them as I would treat Jesus, because He said how I treat them is how I treat Him. I believe it, but I don't like it.

It's easy to love the Jesus whose presence I feel in the music, in nature, or in solitude. But these people? Difficult, hostile, two-faced, scheming against me? It's hard to love them. Only if God intervenes in me can I do it.

One of the best examples of a person who had mastered the art of seeing Jesus in people was Mother Teresa. She once told an interviewer that the poor people she served were

God's greatest gift to her because they allowed her the opportunity "to be twenty-four hours a day with Jesus." And then she said this: "The dying, the crippled, the mentally ill, the unwanted, the unloved—they are Jesus in disguise."[5] Elsewhere she says "Jesus in His *distressing* disguise." It's not Jesus the way you were looking for Him. Will you recognize Him?

I can easily relate to what Barbara Brown Taylor wrote about the difficulty of putting into practice Jesus' ideas about love: "I know that I have an easier time loving humankind than I do loving particular human beings. . . . Particular human beings rarely do things the way I think they should do them, and when they prevent me from doing what I think I should be doing, then I run short on reverence for them."[6]

It's easy to see Jesus in the face of a child, maybe, or even in the face of a hungry homeless person, but how about the clerk at the drive-thru window who messes up your order? Do you feel reverence for that person?

How about the colleague who sends you a scathing e-mail? How about the family member who demands and demands but never gives? Jesus in those people? A very "distressing disguise." "Love *them,*" Jesus says, "and you have loved me."

Taylor said the only remedy for her difficulty is to "pay attention" to these troublesome people even when they are in her way. "Just for a moment," she writes, "I look for the human being instead of the obstacle." She says it's important because "encountering another human being is as close to God as I may ever get—in the eye-to-eye thing, the person-to-person thing—which is where God's beloved promised to show up. Paradoxically, the point is not to see [God]. The point is to see the person standing in front of me, who has no substitute, who can never be replaced, whose heart holds things for which there is no language, whose life is an unsolved mystery."[7]

As we encounter other people, I believe God walks beside us and says, "Look. See these people the way I see them. In your own limited way, learn to love them the way I love them. Get beyond your more self-centered way of thinking of others, and become more like me."

In my own church we recently heard the story of one of our members named Shari who went to the grocery store one day and found an aisle completely blocked by another woman's cart. What do you do when another person is literally blocking your path? Give her a gruff little "Excuse me" and push through? Let out a disgusted sigh? Our church member noticed the young woman had a newborn in her cart. The woman looked frazzled and overwhelmed. She had no idea she was blocking the aisle.

Instead of seeing her as an impediment to her path, Shari started a conversation with her. "How old is your baby?" "Is this your first?" "How are things going?" Shari happened to be the head of our MOPS (Mothers of Preschool Children) program. Before the conversation was over, Shari had invited the woman to come to a MOPS meeting. The woman came and loved it. She also started coming to our church. At the time the two women told their story to the congregation months later, the young mother had been appointed the new head of MOPS. Shari saw Jesus in the form of a harried mother in the grocery aisle that day. Instead of seeing a barrier in her path, she recognized Jesus.

What If Jesus Is Already Here? What the Church Does Right

None of this is to say that Jesus is present in our lives only in the form of people who pose some kind of challenge.

Far from it. One of the places where God's presence is most easily found but also most commonly taken for granted is in a believer's relationships with fellow Christians. What does the Bible call these fellow believers? "The Body of Christ." Such a familiar phrase, but think about its significance. It's not that Jesus is high on a pedestal while the Church is down below gazing up at Him in awe. Instead, He *inhabits* the Church. It's His *body*. If you're in the presence of those fellow believers, you are in His presence.

Many people wish it didn't work that way. Spirituality would be much easier if it could be a matter purely between me and God. He understands me. He brings me joy. He is merciful toward me and my faults.

People, on the other hand, can be annoying. They judge. They frustrate. They misunderstand. They do and say petty things. They plot and scheme and dislike.

Some people want only what they consider the "spiritual" aspects of Christianity, without bothering with the relational side of it. They feel comforted by prayer and Bible reading and music and other religious traditions, but they could do without the people.

Others prefer the opposite. They like the social aspects of being in the church—the lively worship services, dinners, classes, and other gatherings, but they don't want to have to dig too deeply spiritually. Jesus, and the Bible as a whole, teach that His Spirit inhabits *both* the personal spiritual disciplines *and* the relationships with other believers. The kingdom of God, which Jesus ushered in, does not happen in isolation. Jesus sought solitude during His earthly ministry—but only for short periods, and then He was back to His disciples and the crowds.

It's easy to criticize the Church. One of the easiest postures to adopt is to stand slightly off to the side and declare that we disapprove of what the Church has become, how it operates, and how the people in it behave. One reason it's so easy to do that is that so much of the criticism is justified. The Church is flawed, and many of the people in it do stupid and hurtful things. But choosing to be a disciple of Jesus Christ does not include the option of being a critic on the sidelines. Jesus' followers have to dive in with all the other flawed followers and learn how to love each other.

When authors write about the Church, their purpose is often to point out what's wrong with it—understandably so. There are certainly plenty of problems, crises, and disturbing trends. It's better to confront these than to deny them. But step back from the criticism for a moment and consider how many ways, on a day-to-day basis, the Church works. Despite its flaws, every day across the world for countless millions the Church is also serving its function.

Part of my gratitude toward the Church springs from the fact that it welcomed me so lovingly when I first came into contact with it. That was when I was a child, before I had developed criticisms and complaints and excuses for keeping my distance. When my uncle first took me to the church where I became a Christian, I was wary of the whole idea of the church. I went the first time only because I liked my uncle. No one made me go, and no one would have made me return if I hadn't wanted to.

I loved the place, kept coming back, gave my life to Jesus Christ there, became a member, and grew up there because I sensed God's Spirit in that place. The people there embodied God's presence. I couldn't have stated it that way at first, but I knew God was in that place. The evidence was in a thousand details. If you are a Christian, I invite you to take a few minutes right now to list all the ways you can think of—specific moments and examples—of how the Church has embodied God's presence for you.

I sensed Him in the loving welcome I received that first day. I sensed Him in my Sunday School teachers as a kid. I think of my fourth-grade Sunday School teacher, Mrs. De-Long, who offered to buy us a Bible if we memorized six verses of scripture that carried the message of salvation. I memorized the verses—John 3:16, 1 John 1:9, and others—and I vividly remember her taking me out for a soda at a local restaurant and giving me that Bible. I still have it, and those verses are still emblazoned in my memory. God's Spirit suffused that teacher and all my encounters with her.

As a teenager I had my most powerful encounters with God's presence during times when I was with my fellow Christians at church. Teen camps each summer were powerful spiritual high points emotionally and spiritually as my friends and I sang, played, listened, and learned together, committing ourselves to a closer walk with Christ. Youth group meetings, church services, prayer at the altar, struggles with temptations, long talks with friends, discussions with youth pastors—all carried the presence of God powerfully into my life.

After high school as I moved on to college and graduate school and beyond, the people of the Church emerged in each city I lived in to invite me into God's presence. When I moved from Illinois to California to take my current job at Azusa Pacific University, I was single and didn't know anyone in my new hometown except for the people who had interviewed me. With the beginning of the semester still more than six weeks away, I was as alone as I have ever been.

One of the first things I did was find a church. I was a stranger, but they welcomed me, just as Jesus had taught them to do. I made friends there, worshiped the Lord there,

GOD IN THE ORDINARY

and made it my home. I met the woman there who was to become my wife. I got married in the church. Once we had children, we dedicated them in the church.

Sunday School was part of my first encounter with the church at age six. Since then I have taught numerous classes for various ages from kindergarten to single adults to married couples. I became a Christian during a Vacation Bible School at age eight. Since then I have served in several Vacation Bible Schools at different churches. In times of sorrow my church friends have surrounded me. In times of joy my church friends have celebrated with me. They have challenged me, tolerated me, and loved me. I can't imagine how impoverished my life would have been without them.

The way I have been celebrating the Church, however, doesn't tell the whole story. Although I am eternally grateful for the role the Church has played in bringing Christ into my life, I have also spent plenty of time being frustrated, sometimes angry, and sometimes disappointed with the Church. I have also failed the Church and failed to live by Christian values many times over the years. Just as I have experienced love and sacrifice and the undeniable presence of the Holy Spirit among the people of the Church, I have also seen petty behavior, hurtful comments, and destructive attitudes. I've seen people excluded and ignored and insulted. I've seen pastors divide congregations with decisions that seem incomprehensible.

Some of the Church's failures are so devastating that they leave people in pain for years, while others look trivial on the surface but still lead people astray. One time a friend of mine stopped coming to church because one of the older members of the congregation criticized him for how sloppily he dressed. When I heard this, I didn't know who to be more frustrated with—the crusty old man who insulted a fellow congregant over something so ridiculous, or my friend for letting something so trivial drive him away from church. I could give dozens of examples like that from my time in the church, from moral failings to unfulfilled commitments to painful rifts between people. Not only have I *witnessed* such problems, but I have also *caused* them. I stepped into the Church at age six and have been part of it ever since, giving me plenty of time and opportunity to say stupid things, let people down, and hurt people in various ways.

In spite of my flaws, and in spite of the Church's flaws, the Church has stood by me, and I have stood by it. I still believe it is the Body of Christ. I still believe the Holy Spirit infuses it.

Church: The People We're Stuck With, the People We Need

Recently I was reading Tim Stafford's description of Jesus at Gethsemane. Jesus faced the lowest moments of His life as He contemplated His coming betrayal and crucifixion, when everyone would abandon Him to die an excruciatingly painful death. He kept coming back to two things that night as He sought connection with the Father: prayer and friends. That He would turn to prayer during that agonizing night is not surprising; He did that throughout His ministry.

But friends? Everyone who has read the Gethsemane story remembers what happened with the select group of disciples Jesus asked to stay with Him to pray—they fell asleep! On one of the most important nights in history, Jesus asked them to stay awake with Him while He went off a short distance to pray, but they couldn't stay awake even for an hour. Three times Jesus went to pray, and three times He returned to find them asleep. In one sense it's a story of their failure, but in another sense it's a story of how much these friends meant to Jesus. He kept coming back to them, weak though they were. He easily could have gone off to pray alone and not bothered with them, but He wanted them with Him in His time of trouble. He could have given up after one or two of their failures, but He stuck with them anyway.

A few minutes after Jesus returned the third time to find His friends asleep, He endured a far worse treachery. He was betrayed by one of the twelve men closest to Him, Judas. Jesus endured repeated betrayals and failures from His friends, but He never raised the possibility of *not* going through His ordeals with them. Better to have flawed friends than none at all. It's the same with us. We have to expect our friends in the Church to fail us sometimes, just as they failed Jesus. But the idea of the Church, the Body of Christ, is too crucial for us to abandon out of disappointment. Stafford writes,

> The church is not made up of people better than the Twelve. But knowing how those twelve would fail Him, Jesus still leaned on them for strength and comfort as He faced His hardest hour. If we want to be like Him, we will do the same. Like Jesus, we will go back to them twice, even three times, wake them from their sleep and ask, "Will you watch with me?"[8]

Even though I love the Church, I also must admit that I almost always feel a level of discontent with it. I have been fortunate to be part of good churches, but they are never run quite the way I think they should be. Many other Christians in churches all over the world feel that way also, which is fueling the growing trend of dropping out of church altogether or being connected to a church only casually as an occasional attendee who is mostly a critic on the sidelines.

Not long ago I was reading the comments section of an online article discussing the problems of the Church. An older man wrote that he had given up on any participation in his church except for occasional attendance. He claimed that no one cared what he had to say. Despite his years of living as a Christian, no one sought out his wisdom. He could no longer relate to the music that was played or the way people dressed or much of anything else. On Sunday mornings he slipped in and out of the place where he now felt like a stranger.

I sympathize with that man's difficulty handling change, but if he were a member of my church, I think I could show him how to reconnect. I might have a hard time convincing him, though. Whenever I have felt alienated from the people in my church, the best way back to a place where I can love them and experience God's presence there is to practice the spiritual discipline of service. That may not sound as spiritual as the fasting or prayer or other practices associated with spirituality, but it teaches me how to love. "When you do it for the least of these," Jesus says, "you're doing it for me."

Connect with people around you, and you connect with Jesus. The man who withdrew from his church believed no one cared what he had to say, and he may have a legitimate complaint about that. Many churches ignore the wisdom their older members could provide. But in my church, I know there is always work to be done—Sunday School classes that need teachers, children's programs that need volunteers, service projects that need people to make deliveries, worship services that need ushers and greeters, and the list goes on. People may never seek this man out for his wisdom if he is merely sitting in a pew for an hour and then dashing out to his car afterward. But if he's in there serving, getting his hands dirty, interacting with people, mentoring children or teenagers, they're going to listen to him. They'll love and appreciate him, and he may learn to see Jesus in those around him.

I don't mean to exaggerate how service would make this man *feel* about his experience of God's presence or his connection with his church. Serving in the church often doesn't yield the same kind of *emotional* awareness of God's presence that you get from things like listening to inspiring music or sensing Him in the beauty of nature. I sometimes wonder about the people who volunteered for the Vacation Bible School I attended when I became a Christian at age eight. Were those volunteering church members aware that they were leading someone to Christ when they agreed to help? Did they see it as a spiritual practice when they set out the crackers and juice and prepared the crafts and taught the songs?

Or did one of their friends say, "Please help us. We really need you," and they reluctantly agreed? Were they aware of me particularly, or was I just another one of the squirmy kids they had to keep in line until that day's activities ended? Were they relieved when it ended? Whatever their feelings about their service, the Holy Spirit was working in their midst. The life of at least one child was changed forever.

Because I became a Christian in Vacation Bible School, I have sometimes felt drawn to volunteer for VBS in our own church, even though I don't feel I'm all that good with kids that age. I'm used to teaching college students—who know how to sit still. But sometimes I volunteer anyway, and several years ago, when my daughter was six and my son was seven, I volunteered and was the assistant teacher in their class.

The VBS did not go well. The whole week felt like chaos to me, herding these kids from room to room, activity to activity. They talked too much, climbed around on everything, and didn't pay much attention. My own kids were as naughty as any of them. All I kept thinking was, *I can't wait till this is over.*

Then finally it *was* over. As my kids and I were cleaning up the classroom at the end of the final day, I was about to throw away some handouts when my daughter asked if she could have them to play with. So I gave them to her to take home.

Her favorite thing to do was to play teacher, and she would line up about twenty dolls in rows and teach them. She had a whiteboard and a roster and would teach entire lessons to these dolls. The room where I write is next to her bedroom, so that afternoon I was working in my room and Katie was in her room, teaching the dolls. At one point I walked out in the hall and looked into her room. Every doll had a VBS handout. Katie was having a heart-to-heart talk with them.

The entire chaotic VBS we had just endured took on a whole new meaning to me when I heard Katie say this: "You know, if you sin Jesus will forgive you."

I stood there amazed as my daughter shared the gospel, the real gospel, to this roomful of dolls. And I thought, *When did she learn this?* I just spent the whole week trying to get her to quiet down, sit down, pay attention, throw her trash away, keep her hands to herself. I didn't think she got any spiritual content out of that VBS. I had thought of it as pretty much a wasted week. I thought of all the work I could have gotten done if I weren't chasing those kids around. Yet somehow my daughter had learned the core of Christianity so well that she could now teach it to her dolls. The Holy Spirit was among us the whole time, I now believe. He shows up when we serve one another. When someone like Mother Teresa says that being with the poor means that she gets to spend every day with Jesus, that isn't just a sentimental euphemism for work that is unpleasant. He really is there, even though He looks and feels much different than we expected.

Go to beaconhillbooks.com for a free downloadable study guide that includes questions for deeper personal reflection as well as activities for use in a small-group setting.

six ⊠ ⊠ ⊠

GOD IN THE ORDINARY
He Dances in the Music

■ My earliest memory of sensing God's Spirit is hearing Him in music.

From childhood until now, I have always loved to put on my headphones, turn the music up loud, and dance and sing in celebration of God's presence. Unlike study of the Bible or other spiritual disciplines, which I had to be taught, worshiping God through music came naturally. It was simply the best and most enjoyable way to draw close to Him. The songs and music styles pouring through those headphones changed over the years, but those things didn't matter much to me. I love rock music. I love hymns. I love any music that draws me into God's presence.

When I stayed with my grandmother as a boy, she liked to tell people how I would stand in a corner of her living room, open up her hymnal, and pretend to be the music leader at her church. I asked the congregation to turn to page six (always that page, for some reason), and sing whatever hymn I happened to remember. Before I could ever understand a sermon, I could understand the Holy Spirit in the hymns. I loved listening to the blending of voices, the instruments, the outpouring of praise from the congregation. I believed God hovered close to us as we sang, clapped our hands, and let the music swirl around us. I still believe that.

Why Words Alone Fall Flat

Why music? For conveying *information* about the faith, music falls far short of other modes of worship, such as sermons or Bible studies. Some songs convey inspiring theological truths through the beauty of their words—think of songs like Charles Wesley's "And Can It Be?" or Keith Getty and Stuart Townend's "In Christ Alone." But with most modern worship songs and even with more traditional hymns, it takes words and music together to create the power of the experience. Music is not primarily information. It is experience, it is spirit, it is emotion.

Words are powerful, but they are not enough. Words alone cannot contain the full reality of God's presence. Even the most soaring and transcendent music can only hint at God's grandeur, of course, but music magnifies words in ways that help them come closer, given human limitations, to conveying the glory of God.

Music not only allows us to get closer to the depth of our love and worship of God than we can achieve through words alone, but it also is a vehicle for God to commune with us. In Psalm 22:3 David writes of God, "Yet you are holy, enthroned on the praises of Israel" (ESV). Another translation describes God as "dwelling in the praises" of Israel, and the King James Version says God "inhabitest the praises" of Israel. The Holy Spirit inhabits the music. We don't simply sing to Him. He meets with us in the surge of sound and praise.

My own sense of God's presence in the music has been so strong since I was a child that when I wrote my first book, a fantasy novel called *Song of Fire*, I created a world in which music is the most powerful force on the planet. God's Spirit inhabits the music so powerfully in that place that music is not only sound but also light.

When the main character, Jeremy, first arrives in the place, he descends "in a swirl of music so bright" he can't see anything else around him. Each sound has its own appearance, each bit of light its own sound. He not only hears and sees the sound, but it also carries him physically. As he describes the experience,

At what must have been millions of miles per hour, I pierced through a melody that was faster and more complicated and glorious than any sound my ears had ever been able to hear. As I sliced through the music, it pierced through me like bolts of energy. Every cell in my body tingled with power, with the very Spirit of God. I never wanted to leave the music. I wrapped myself in it, flung myself thousands of miles through it, sang in it, danced in it.

Jeremy can change the music any way he wants to, slowing it down, making it louder or quieter, adding variations, just by thinking it. The other instruments follow whatever he does and surprise him with variations of their own "as if we were speaking to one another in some elaborate language."[1] Music obliterates any sense of time. It takes him out of himself and makes him forget his surroundings.

God's Spirit is so powerful in the music that the enemies of God's people in that place outlaw it and do everything they can to wipe it out. Wars are fought over it. If people truly experience God's presence, which inhabits the music, there will be no way for His enemies to keep people away from Him.

The music in *Song of Fire* is made up—but just barely. Music is so imbued with God's presence that it often feels as if it *should* possess the physical properties it has in the novel. It *should* burst forth not only in sound but also in light. I *should* be able to see all those intertwining strands of light and sound shooting off into the atmosphere. I *should* be able to physically ride the waves of sound at the speed of the song. I wonder whether such things will be possible in eternity. I wonder whether the music we have now, as glorious as it is, is muted. Our music is a foretaste of the music of heaven, but we hear it and also sing it and play it through the fallen world's static, as if we were trying to listen to a symphony on an AM station on an old tinny transistor radio.

Music is not only a way for God's Spirit to reach us but also a way for us to express our love and awe of Him. I'm glad we have more than simply words for that purpose. As a writer and literature teacher, I appreciate the power of words, but I also know that words are too limited to capture the vastness of spiritual reality. Words have a precision and a level of detail that help to dissect the nuances of *ideas*, but they can be inadequate to capture the immensity of some of the concepts they point to.

It's one thing, for instance, to *say* the words "Hallelujah, for the Lord God omnipotent reigneth. And He shall reign forever and ever." Good words. I understand the meaning. But it falls a little flat. When a choir sings those words in Handel's *Messiah*, accompanied by an orchestra, the music soars and gives a truer sense of the magnificent reality those words convey.

I remember the first time I heard the "Hallelujah Chorus." I was a child, and our choir sang it on Easter Sunday morning in church. I didn't know about the tradition of standing during the song, a practice that reportedly started when the beauty of the music led King George II to stand as he heard it for the first time in the eighteenth century. When everyone stood up that Easter Sunday morning when I first heard the song, I was thrilled, because standing was exactly what I wanted to do. God inhabited our praise that morning. I had a foretaste of what I believe the music of eternity will be.

Sapping the Power of the Sound

Unfortunately, the power of "The Hallelujah Chorus" has faded for me. Now I'm most likely to hear little snippets of it in commercials, with the "hallelujah" celebrating the advent of a new denture cream or an improved laundry detergent or some other product to solve some minor concern of modern consumer living. Much of the music in our day has been sapped of its power by its trivial overuse. A fragment of a song bursts forth from a cell phone to indicate a call is coming in. Is that music? Can that in any way be a satisfying use of a song you love?

I walked through a shopping mall recently and was overwhelmed by all the competing music bombarding me from every direction. As one tune played in the mall corridor, most of the individual stores also blasted their own songs, which mixed with the competing songs to form an ugly cacophony. No one paid much attention to any of it anyway. If anything, most of the customers tried to block out the noise so they could pay attention to what their friends were saying or so they could concentrate on what they were buying. For some, this is now what music is, background sound to keep the dreaded silence at bay.

Personally, I would rather have real music, delivered in a way that I can hear and experience it, or have silence. Silence offers a chance to think, to pray, to hold conversations with people, to hear the sounds of the world around me. If I have been without music for a time, then when I do hear it I can actually *hear* it and feel its richness and beauty. When I wander through a world filled with music as wallpaper, overheard scraps of other people's electronic noise, then my soul gradually deadens even to the sound of real music. I don't want to let it lose its power. It can mean far more than most people let it.

Music That Leads You into God's Presence

Music can move us closer to the thin boundary that separates us from the spiritual realm. Psalm 150 says, "Praise God in his sanctuary; praise him in his mighty heavens." It calls for praising God with trumpets and the harp and lyre and strings and flutes and tambourines and cymbals. John Koessler writes that we often mistakenly think of worship as beginning on earth and moving toward heaven, but Psalm 150 shows it starting in God's heavenly sanctuary and then resounding throughout the earth. It brings the two together. "Let everything that has breath praise the LORD" (Psalm 150:6). Koessler quotes Jonathan Edwards, who said that "the church on earth is the same society with those saints who are praising God in heaven. There is not one church of Christ in heaven and another here upon earth." When we worship God, Koessler says, we are engaging in "a heavenly activity. The worshiping church does not merely imitate what goes on in heaven. It participates in heaven's worship. We take up a theme that was begun by others before the throne of God, adding our voices to theirs."[2] Like many other Christians, I have been in services that have felt much like what I imagine heaven will be. Maybe these times feel that way because heaven and earth join together during that kind of worship, and the barrier between the two is so thin that it almost disappears entirely.

It's easy to think of music in a worship service as merely part of the introductory material leading to the sermon, like announcements or the offering. It's also easy to think of it as little more than religious entertainment, a pleasant diversion to go along with the serene atmosphere of the sanctuary. It should be far more. Music can bring a congregation together, creating a sense of unity that may happen at few other times.

Music can also be a crucial part of our individual times of prayer and worship. In every church I have ever been part of, the pastors and Sunday school teachers have stressed the importance of regular personal times of Scripture reading and prayer. I believe in that and practice it, but I also often add music, an element that is seldom mentioned when people talk of a personal devotional time. I know many people who *intend* to set aside time for prayer and Bible reading and who believe it's important for maintaining a close relationship with God, but they find themselves neglecting it anyway. Why? The most common reason is they say they're too busy, but I wonder whether that's really the problem.

When I have a hectic day ahead of me, or when I've just finished a tough day, the thought of reading the next portion of Scripture on the list as I make my way through the Bible can seem like one more chore to get through. Scripture reading and prayer draw on the intellectual side of our faith more than the relational and emotional side. Some days I simply want to spend time with God, enjoy His presence. That's what music helps me do. Prayer comes as I sit and listen to the worship songs that usher me into His presence.

As I sing and listen, I find myself feeling released from the pressures of the day rather than feeling that I added one more task to the list. I go away feeling closer to God and can face life with a greater sense of love and balance. Sometimes when I'm working on a big writing project or other task, I take a break from it and turn on some music so I can dance and sing and celebrate God's Spirit. It can be inspiring and invigorating and fun. I return to the hard work energized and content.

When Music Divides

Music as I have described it sounds like an undeniably joyful and positive gift from God, but unfortunately, music in the Church can also spark conflict so severe that it sometimes splits congregations. Battles dubbed "worship wars" pit those who favor traditional hymns against proponents of contemporary worship songs. Traditionalists accuse the other side of abandoning the theologically rich heritage of hymns that have inspired the Church for hundreds of years, while those who favor contemporary songs accuse traditionalists of holding the church back from creating worship services that will be relevant for younger believers and non-Christian seekers. A music minister I know regularly received nasty letters from members of the congregation when the church in which he served transitioned from a more traditional to a more contemporary music style.

Although it is disturbing to think that something as inspiring and beautiful as music could become a catalyst for division and pettiness, I think that happens because people feel so profoundly connected to the music they love. Their enthusiasm can turn destructive if they fear that this music is threatened. Because the Lord's presence touches people so profoundly through music, Christians come to love and even idealize those songs through which they encountered Him. It's easy to mistakenly believe the songs themselves are the source of the power rather than the Holy Spirit who inhabits them. If someone threatens to remove those songs from the church, it can feel as if he or she is threatening to remove God himself. God speaks through those songs! How could anyone think of replacing them? Especially with this other drivel that isn't nearly as good. Time to fight!

Some Christian songs are so bad that I cringe whenever we have to sing them in church. I won't mention examples, because the ones I'm thinking of are likely someone else's favorites. That's the trouble with music. Our responses to what is good and bad are so personal, but also so deeply felt, that it's hard to come to a consensus about what will be conducive to worship for an entire congregation. To me, some songs are so obviously *good*, so obviously anointed by the Holy Spirit, that it seems clear that anyone with the gift of hearing would agree that our congregation should sing them as often as possible. Yet people I know and love—including my own children—can't stand those songs. What's wrong with these people?

This division over music isn't limited to the Church, of course. I never could understand why my parents didn't like the rock music I listened to on the car radio or blasted from the stereo in my bedroom. In the car they kept changing the station from my "good" music to their country music, and my sister and I had to sit there and endure it (though now for some reason those old country songs they liked don't seem so bad to me anymore). Similarly, I can hardly stand the dreck my own children listen to on the radio.

When we're talking about the casual pleasure of listening to music on the radio, it's often easier for people to chalk up their musical differences with other people as simply a matter of taste. She likes country, he likes rock, the neighbor likes opera. In those cases, people are not as likely to make an argument against the music they don't like. They simply would rather not listen to it. I do remember some adults saying about the rock music I liked as a teenager, "That's not music. That's just noise." Offensive lyrics can also be a matter for dispute, but most differences are a matter of style and preference, and people realize that. If you like jazz but I don't, that doesn't cause a rift between us.

With hymns and other worship music, however, the connections to people's deep spiritual memories and associations make it more difficult to dismiss the differences so casually. If I believe you want to take away the music in which I have experienced the very presence of the Lord, I might be tempted to question not only your wisdom but also your spiritual commitment. It might be easy for me to quickly move from "I don't like the music you're trying to make me accept" to "This is not of the Lord" or "This is of the devil" or "You're ruining the church with this garbage."

What the Worship Warriors Can Learn from Each Other

People on various sides of the worship music debate have much to learn from each another. What a horrible loss to the Church if it were to cast aside hundreds of years of theologically rich, soul-shaking hymns simply because popular musical tastes have shifted! Is the Church so narrow that it cannot draw from a range of traditions and styles and combine the best of all of them? Do congregants, no matter what their age or tastes or background, really value only music that is new? As T. David Gordon, author of *Why Johnny Can't Sing Hymns*, said in an interview with Mark Moring, "Many are promoting an 'aesthetic' that it is our duty to patronize living artists and not artists who are dead. Should we also not read books that are more than fifty years old or not enter buildings that are more than fifty years old? We haven't rejected other art forms that are not new. We've done so only with music."[3]

Gordon makes a good point that Christians in our generation seem willing to discard older music more quickly and casually than they would discard other art forms. We borrow that idea about music's short shelf life, I believe, largely from the way popular culture treats music. On the radio, a song that came out ten years ago is an "oldie." When I hear songs that were popular on the radio when I was a teenager, they seem ancient. However, I don't have that same feeling about most books from that era or even much older. C. S. Lewis wrote books in the 1950s and earlier, but they still seem fresh. When I teach American literature, anything from the twentieth century to the present seems recent. Songs from those same eras feel old. People who might eagerly read works written centuries ago by Chaucer or Shakespeare might be reluctant to play something so "old" as a big band album from the 1940s.

I worship in a church that no longer uses hymnals. I recently had to explain to my twelve-year-old daughter what a hymnal *is*. I'm old enough to remember when hymns were the dominant music style in church, but I'm young enough to enjoy contemporary Christian music. I've been content with whatever style the church chose. I've not been a warrior in the "worship wars." But as I write this, I pulled an old hymnal off my bookshelf to see how much difference it really makes to me that this music has mostly been set aside. In our church we do still sing some hymns in a more contemporary style, with words projected onto a screen.

From the first few pages alone, I feel shaken by the power of these great songs. The first hymn is "How Firm a Foundation," followed by "Joyful, Joyful, We Adore Thee," "To God Be the Glory," "A Mighty Fortress Is Our God," "How Great Thou Art!" and "O Worship the King." I set the book down as these hymns play in my mind. Their depth and power are astounding, but my own children and most of the younger members of our church wouldn't recognize most of them. I flip through the rest of the book, and I ache for what we have given up: "All Hail the Power of Jesus' Name," "Love Divine, All Loves Excelling," "My Jesus, I Love Thee," "He Hideth My Soul," "Day by Day," "Come, Thou Fount," "I Am Thine, O Lord," and many others. Even skimming, I don't get through a third of the book before I stop and set it aside, too discouraged to dwell any further on these abandoned songs.

Hymns are often discarded from contemporary worship services because worship leaders believe contemporary audiences can no longer relate to that music style, but Christian composer and music professor Lawrence Mumford points out that worshipers may be more eclectic in their tastes than people think. Although these contemporary audiences may listen to pop music all week on the radio, they also enjoy other styles. For example, they hear a great deal of film music, which is a much different style than what they hear on the radio. Musical theater is popular even though it draws from a variety of styles, and many churchgoers attend concerts at local schools and other venues where classical and other musical styles are featured. "In short," he writes, "the pop song genre is certainly not the only music that any churchgoer hears, absorbs, or even enjoys between weekend services."[4] In other words, people may be more willing than we think to worship God in a variety of musical styles.

Some Christian musicians are moving beyond hymns or contemporary worship choruses to explore different ways of using music to lead people into God's presence and to help them reflect on Him and His creation. The style is sometimes called "post-rock," and Joel Hartse describes it this way: "While these bands use rock instruments and the occasional horn or string section, they have more in common with classical music, building long, symphonic compositions with swelling emotional climaxes."[5] Played by groups such as Hammock, Foxhole, Immanu El, and others, this music is mostly wordless and slow, and the songs are longer than the typical three- or four-minute contemporary worship song. The aim in worship services that use such music is to create an atmosphere of reverence and to "offer an opportunity for the co-creation of a worship experience shared by listener, performer and Holy Spirit alike."

No one but the enemy of our soul wins if music becomes a battleground for Christians rather than a force that brings them together. Music offers a foretaste of eternity like few other gifts on the planet. It can draw us close to the thinnest part of the veil that separates our world from the heavenly realm. Styles and tastes may change over the generations, but the Holy Spirit keeps speaking through this ineffable language.

Go to beaconhillbooks.com for a free downloadable study guide that includes questions for deeper personal reflection as well as activities for use in a small-group setting.

seven ☒ ☒ ☒
GOD IN THE ORDINARY
He Astonishes the Intellect

■ Is your intellect capable of love?

We know the intellect is capable of many other great things—it can pursue truth, ponder new ideas, propose and test hypotheses, invent new technologies, solve problems, contemplate abstract ideas, and create works of literature, architecture, and art. But love?

When you think of how you approach relationships—with a romantic partner, with friends, with God—how big a part does the intellect play in bringing you together? In popular songs and romantic movies, the intellect is often portrayed as antithetical to love. You "fall" in love rather than calculate your careful descent into it. Love is "blind," not logical and discerning. In romantic comedies, the audience doesn't side with those who think through relationships rationally and do what makes the most sense. Instead, the hero or heroine eventually tosses logic aside—at whatever cost—for the promise of love.

"Love the Lord your God with all your heart and with all your soul and with all your mind," Jesus said in Matthew

22:37. He places the mind on an equal basis with the heart and soul. Sadly for many Christians today, the church is a place where they can pretty much set aside their intellect. The intellect may play a big part in their work or in other endeavors, but their church appeals to heart and soul almost exclusively.

In churches like this the intellect is suspect because it is too often associated with things people don't like—pedantic know-it-alls who use their knowledge as a weapon against others, nerdy misfits who take refuge in mental minutia, dull practitioners of a dried-out faith of stale words. These churches find it much safer to keep things friendly and light. A certain amount of intellect is necessary for the church members to understand enough Scripture and doctrine to get them saved, but appeals to belief and emotion are what really propel the congregation. Tone down the intellectual stuff, they think, or it will turn people off.

Such a narrow view of the intellect is, of course, not what Jesus is talking about at all. To get a sense of why the mind is as crucial as the heart and soul in loving God, we need to sweep away prejudices that have led people to wall off their intellectual life from their faith. The intellect can open us to God's presence in ways that no other faculty can replace. To shut it off or to diminish its place in our spiritual life is to cut off a crucial way of loving God and knowing the joy of His presence.

What kills the appeal of the intellect for many people is the seemingly *obligatory* nature of it. In other words, it's something they think they *should* engage more fully, but the truth is—they find it dull. They associate it with homework and exams and other things they do because they *have* to even though they would rather not. They know they should engage the intellect more, just as they should finish those math problems or complete that essay for English class, but they'll be glad when it's over. This view of the intellect equates it with mental drudgery. No wonder people who hold that perception have trouble seeing what it has to do with loving God.

A Lesson from a Fish

The idea of loving God with your intellect is not a "do your homework" message. It's not a matter of trying to force yourself to become smarter or making yourself memorize more Bible verses. Instead, it's a matter of awakening to the pleasure and inspiration and spiritual food the intellect already offers. To get a little closer to how the mind may bring us into a more joyful and loving relationship with God, I'll start with my goldfish. His name was Jaws, and he was our only pet. He died a couple months ago after living a little more than a year in his bowl in our home. He was my son's fish originally, the prize at a carnival game, but somehow I ended up being the one who took care of him. I fed him and cleaned his bowl every day.

Jaws had his good points—he had a beautiful color, he grew as the months went by, he was a good swimmer, and he was a good listener. He wasn't much when it came to the intellect, though. His routine was to swim around the bowl, eat, and make a mess. The next day he did the same thing. Maybe a fish doesn't want much more than that. I don't know, because he couldn't tell me. I couldn't help but feel sorry for him. The universe outside that bowl was filled with millions of books, ideas, creatures, planets, suns, cities, mountains, oceans, music, movies, and experiences of every kind.

His world was a bowl. He swam and ate.

Not his fault. We put him into the bowl. But even if we had set him free in a pond or creek, his world would still have been pretty limited.

So what? Jaws was a goldfish. None of them have much of an intellectual life, and their mental and physical limitations mean they never will. They're missing out on vast amounts of the fascinating and meaningful ideas and experiences life has to offer, but they don't know it. Maybe they have a kind of contentment in their ignorance. Maybe they think they're already experiencing all the good things reality has to offer.

They make me think of all the people who voluntarily limit themselves to a kind of intellectual goldfish bowl. Within sight of their limited daily routine is a thrilling universe they ignore. The fish at least have the excuse that they can't get out of the bowl. People could, but they choose not to. A richer, deeper knowledge of God and His creation is within their grasp, but they won't lift their hand to take it. For those of us who teach, one of the questions from students we hate the most is "Do I *have* to know this?" The implication of that question is that the student wants nothing more in his or her brain than what absolutely *has* to be there to get a certain grade. Why not? The extra knowledge is there for the taking.

I realize taking the knowledge requires some effort, and life has many demands, and nobody can know everything. Given the information-overloaded world we live in, we all have to make decisions about what to let into our minds and what to keep out. But many people have trapped themselves in far too small a fishbowl. They have cut off their awareness, if they ever had it, of the rewards to be gained from *knowing* more, from experiencing the jolt of joy that can come from knowledge. It is possible to know God and

His creation better, but many Christians close off at least some of the doors that could lead to deeper love and a more vivid sense of His presence.

Does the Bible Help Us *Know* God, or Know *About* Him?

Why do Christians close those doors to knowledge? Part of it can simply be laziness or being too busy or other simple excuses like that, but the reasons can also be more subtle. Consider one obvious type of knowledge that can lead people to a deeper understanding of God: reading the Bible. I can't think of any Christian I know who would dispute the fact that reading Scripture is a good idea, but I can think of many Christians I know who rarely do it. Why?

For many, they have never experienced the Bible in a way that brings it to life. Their perception of it gets stuck at thinking of the Bible as a difficult and rather confusing book that should be *revered* as God's Word and should be read in order to prove you're serious about being a Christian. It teaches things about God, of course, and about His expectations and doctrine. But beyond providing knowledge *about* God, can it really help a Christian *know* God?

What I most want to say about the Bible is this: It will change you.

God simply uses Scripture in ways that He uses nothing else to reach you and teach you and make you more like Him. It won't happen if you merely think highly of the Bible or carry it with you to church or display it prominently in your home—or read a few verses here and there when directed to do so during a sermon. But I firmly believe that if you *immerse* yourself in it and open your mind and heart and soul to it, you will find God's presence there. You will know Him in a way you have never known Him before.

People resist the Bible, and in one sense it's not hard to see why. For a modern reader it can be daunting. The way it tells stories and presents information is simply not the way we do it anymore. Some portions are reader-friendly, but others are not, such as the long lists of rules in Deuteronomy, the visionary and complex prophecies in Isaiah and Revelation, the genealogies scattered throughout several books, the histories of obscure kings and battles, and many other examples.

Even when the Bible is recounting stories, where a modern reader might expect to feel on more solid footing, they are often not our kinds of stories. They're sometimes truncated and lacking in some of the key elements of plot and character and exposition that we're used to today. One of the literature textbooks I use in a course I teach includes the biblical story of Lot's wife, who is turned into a pillar of salt as she looks back in the escape from the destruction of Sodom and Gomorrah. One question I pose to the students is what elements the biblical story deletes that a modern writer would include. The Bible doesn't tell her name, doesn't give her motive for why she turned back, doesn't explain why she was turned into a pillar of salt. *Why pillar? Why salt?* We get one verse about her, and then the story goes on. Modern poets, whose work is also included in the textbook, have written about her to fill in those gaps with their own speculation.

Still, as unusual as the Bible is for modern readers, God overcomes those barriers and meets people who read it, as He has done for centuries. Scripture is not the *only* way of knowing God, of course, but it opens a door to an understanding of Him that many Christians leave closed.

The intimacy one can find with God through His Word can be illustrated by a similar dynamic that happens when readers get to "know" an author through his or her liter-ary works. For many people, the great authors in literary history—Shakespeare, Twain, Hemingway, Chaucer, Wolfe, Homer, Eliot, Frost—are little more than names they vague-ly remember from a class they were forced to take in school. They may remember a few lines of the works or some plot details from the stories, but the writers remain distant fig-ures, respected but unapproachable. For many students encountering the works of these writers for the first time, the experience can be intimidating. The language itself may be forbidding as the reader struggles to move from his or her own world into the author's distant world and way of thinking. As they do with Scripture, some readers give it a try, fulfill whatever assignment they have been forced to do, and then set it aside. In the minds of those readers, the author remains more of a marble statue than a real person with captivating ideas that can reach across centuries and grip a reader's soul.

The God of the Bible is as out of reach as those dusty classic authors for many people, but it doesn't have to be that way. Do you have a favorite author in whose works you have immersed yourself to the point that you feel you know that writer almost as well as you know your own family and friends? Can you think of an author who, if that per-son walked into your room right now, you feel you could sit down with and feel a stronger connection than you feel with many of the people you see every day?

For me, Thomas Wolfe, an American novelist who died in 1938, is such an author. When I first read his novel *Look Homeward, Angel*, I was blown away by the power of it. I felt a strong identification with him and his characters. I felt that this was an author who knew what life is really like. I immediately picked up another of his novels and started in. Later, I was able to visit the home where he grew up and where much of his fiction is set. It was like walking into the book itself. Chills went through me as I walked from room to room and remembered the scenes that took place there. Part of me expected the characters to walk through the doorway at any moment and start living the lives I had read about.

In graduate school I decided to write my dissertation on Wolfe. Further study of his novels and short stories revealed layers and layers of meaning that I had missed in my first enthusiasm. I joined the Thomas Wolfe Society and attended conferences about his work at places that were significant in his life. It's been more than twenty years since I finished my dissertation, but I'm still reading and writing about Wolfe. The more I learn, the more questions are raised, and the more research I want to pursue.

The layers of meaning and revelations in the Bible are far greater than any scholar could find in Wolfe or any other novelist. I have known many biblical scholars and lifelong Bible readers, but I have never met anyone, no matter how much he or she has studied or memorized Scripture, who says that he or she has gotten to the bottom of it. No one says of the Bible, "Oh, yes—I read that book and figured it all out. Time to move on to the next thing." Like other great literature, it keeps revealing layer after layer of truth and knowledge of God.

But there is a difference between the Bible and other literature. When you immerse yourself in the works of a great author, you feel as if you know him or her, but you really don't. The author wouldn't know who you were if he or she walked into the room. But with the Bible, it's more like receiving a letter or e-mail from a friend. You really *do* know that person, and you sense the person within the words of that message. You can also *really* know God and sense His Spirit in the words that will teach you, change you, and bring you closer to Him. As countless Christians will attest, God makes himself known through His Word. He speaks through it. He inhabits it.

Unfortunately, not all Christians experience the Bible that way. Though they may be passionate believers, if they were honest they would really have to admit that they're a little bored with the Bible. They might have a few favorite verses, and they believe Scripture is true, but they don't want to spend much time with it.

Often the reason for that indifference or boredom with Scripture is that they have only nibbled at it. They get a morsel of it in a sermon, a snippet in a Sunday School class, a verse or two on a poster or brochure, a sprinkling of it in worship songs. They've heard stories from it since they were a kid in Sunday School, so they sort of feel like they know it, and they let that be enough.

Hearing portions of it taught in sermons and Bible studies is helpful, but that isn't enough. The Bible is not easy, and finding the depth of its meaning will not come without effort. But for whatever reason, God has chosen to use this book to make himself known to people. I don't know why He does it this way. In many ways it is a very strange and unwieldy book, a conglomeration of history, poetry, parables, genealogies, letters, biographies, prophecies, and other genres of writing, written by different authors over a span of hundreds of years, somehow fitting together to tell the story of God's activity in human affairs and pointing the way to salvation. There is no shortcut to experiencing its power. God will reveal himself to you through it, but He does so as you read it day after day, book after book, immersing yourself not only in the words but also in prayer and reflection.

One of the best ways I've found to help me immerse myself in Scripture rather than simply dabble in it is to follow a read-the-Bible-in-a-year schedule, which is published in many Bibles and elsewhere. Often it takes me longer than a year to finish the schedule, as I slow down on certain parts or miss some days of reading. The timing is not as important as the fact that I'm moving through the entirety of the Bible, letting it sink deep. I make this reading part of my time of prayer. I invite God to speak to me through His Word. I also study the Bible with other believers in a small-group class at my church and listen carefully to the commentary of our Bible-oriented pastor as he preaches from the Word. I also read the works of other Christian authors who reflect on Scripture. The cumulative effect of this exposure to the Bible is that the book ceases to be a distant and forbidding historical artifact and instead becomes a living document through which the Holy Spirit connects with me.

When God Uses Scripture Miraculously

I wish I could describe the way the Bible works differently from any other book. God's surprising ways of using Scripture stood out in an especially vivid way when I was researching *God in Pursuit* and came across story after story in which the Bible had been the key tipping point that moved someone toward faith in Jesus Christ. The surprising part was that the people for whom the Bible played such a central role were often people who had little previous experience with Scripture. Although the Bible seems so daunting to many who first encounter it, in these stories the Holy Spirit broke through that barrier of understanding and brought them to salvation with no other outside guidance.

Mary Kay Beard was once on the FBI's Ten Most Wanted list. She was sentenced to twenty-one years in prison for armed robbery and grand larceny. Desperate for anything that might ease the sense that her life was over, one day she took out the Gideon-placed prison Bible that had been issued to her and that she kept under her pillow. She flipped through the pages and landed on a passage in Ezekiel: "I will give you a new heart and put a new spirit in you; I will remove from you your heart of stone and give you a heart of flesh. And I will put my Spirit in you and move you to follow my decrees and be careful to keep my laws" (Ezekiel 36:26-27). This one passage got hold of her, and the Holy Spirit spoke through it. She kept thinking about this passage and even diagrammed the sentences the way she had been taught to do in school. She longed for the new heart and new spirit the verses promised. She prayed at the edge of her bunk and turned her life over to God.[1]

Why would God use the Bible in this way to reach someone? Flipping through the Bible and grabbing a couple of verses out of context seems the opposite of what good Bible study calls for. And there are plenty of other ways she could have first been led to Christ—the friendship and witness of other Christians, a sermon in a church, and so on. Instead, God used His Word as the first turning point. In the two years after her conversion, Beard did study Scripture more intensely, reading the Bible eight times in its entirety. After her early release from prison, she founded the popular Angel Tree program, part of Charles Colson's Prison Fellowship ministry.

Beard's story may sound like a fluke, but as I researched conversions, I ran across many such stories of how one verse of Scripture was the spark that led to belief in Christ. Charles G. Finney, who eventually became one of the most influential preachers of the nineteenth century, didn't even have to *read* the Scripture that led to his transformation. He said that as he struggled in prayer for forgiveness, "This passage of Scripture seemed to drop into my mind with a flood of light: 'Then shall ye go and pray unto me, and I will hearken unto you. Then shall ye seek me and find me, when ye shall search for me with all your heart.'" Finney said he "knew that that was a passage of Scripture, though I do not think I had ever read it. I knew that it was God's word, and God's voice, as it were, that spoke to me."[2]

The Bible remains relevant throughout our lives, no matter how many times we have read it, because the Holy Spirit continues to speak through it no matter where we are in our faith. He speaks through Scripture in times of crisis, doubt, questioning, and celebration. When we are fearful, Scripture can calm us; when we need comfort, His words can soothe; when we have fallen into sin, His Word can guide us back to forgiveness. Many Christians could transform their faith by taking the one step of delving into the Bible and opening their minds to the Holy Spirit. Yet for many, the Bible remains untouched on a shelf.

The Intellect Can Liberate and Inspire

While the Bible is a crucial way for Christians to love God with their minds, it certainly isn't the only way. God created the world, and pushing ourselves out of the narrow confines in which we sometimes get stuck and venturing into the world of ideas can bring us closer to Him if we let it. I feel fortunate to work at a university where the ideas are spinning everywhere across campus. I walk through hallways and hear snippets of lectures and discussions on psychology, math, literature, history, nursing, and every other imaginable topic. Throughout the school year we are invited

104

to hear guest lecturers, poets, musicians, theologians, and artists. Our students put on plays, perform concerts, and engage in sports of every kind. Not all of this has specifically religious content, but it's part of my spiritual life anyway. It's part of how I love God with my mind.

Even in a university as dynamic as ours, some students narrow their view of it so much that they see it only as a job training center. They see it as a place where a certain number of credits have to be accumulated in order to graduate. How much richer their experience could be if they treated the university as a place that reveals the universe and thus reveals God!

Some Christians are more naturally inclined toward the life of the mind, so loving God through their intellect comes more easily to them. Dorothy L. Sayers, a committed Christian whose works have influenced countless readers, wrote this of her strong inclination toward experiencing God through the intellect: "Since I cannot come at God through intuition, or through my emotions, or through my 'inner light' . . . there is only the intellect left. . . . It is the only point at which ecstasy can enter. I do not know whether we can be saved by the intellect, but I do know that I can be saved by nothing else."[3]

Few people I know, even among those who are intellectually inclined, would go that far. Most Christians approach God not only through intellect but also through intuition, emotion, music, nature, relationships, and other ways. But I also know Christians who move too far in the opposite direction, adopting an anti-intellectualism they may think is more spiritual than Sayers' approach. When they see someone dancing and singing in a worship service with hands raised, or when they hear a simple and direct sermon that anyone can grasp, they believe they are in the presence of

real faith. But they are suspicious of a quieter, more cere-
bral Christian who seeks God in reflection or in scholarly
research or in wrestling with an intellectual conundrum
of the faith. The zeal of these more thought-oriented Christians is powerful but *less visible*, which may make some of
their more extroverted fellow believers assume it isn't real.

Some passionate believers may downplay the intellect
because they are afraid it may lead to an austere, sterile
practice of Christianity that is about ideas only and not
about a true, powerful encounter with the living God. They
stress *relationship* with God and other believers over a carefully argued defense of the faith or wide-ranging Christian
exploration of *all* areas of the universe God has created.

This strain of anti-intellectualism creates a false either/
or choice. Intellect doesn't preclude passion. Intellect doesn't
diminish the role of relationship in the Christian faith. The
Church needs brilliant scholars and intellectuals just as
it needs people passionate about homeless ministries and
rousing worship services and every other aspect of the
Church. Part of the strength of the Church is that its members approach their faith with different natural gifts. These
differences are a cause for celebration, not suspicion. As
Paul taught, the Church is like a human body, and "if the
whole body were an eye, where would the sense of hearing
be? If the whole body were an ear, where would the sense
of smell be? But in fact God has arranged the parts in the
body, every one of them, just as he wanted them to be" (1
Corinthians 12:17-18).

Christians often misunderstand other believers who approach their faith with an emphasis on gifts and interests
that are different from their own. It is also easy for people
to become unbalanced in their own faith when they lean so
heavily on their own favored aspect of the Christian life that

they ignore the other aspects. In Dennis P. Hollinger's book *Head, Heart & Hands: Bringing Together Christian Thought, Passion and Action,* he shows the danger of that unbalance when, for example, service and ministry are extolled but the intellect is shoved aside, or when transcendence and prayer are revered but relationships with other believers are neglected. Anti-intellectual Christians, which he calls "headless Christians," usually "resort to a faith dominated by feelings alone and become spiritually dependent on their own emotional state or on a series of peak 'spiritual experiences.' . . . Without the mind, faith will not be sustained, for it will lack a compass, a grounded worldview and the motivations and sustaining guidance necessary for life's challenges and disappointments."[4]

Not all Christians will or should become scholars, but even those whose interests and gifts lie in other areas of the faith can still have a vibrant intellectual life in which they love God with all their minds. If the Church is functioning properly, the Christian scholars and thinkers will help spread the beauty of the intellect across the entire Church rather than restricting it to a narrow group of insiders. The Church needs Christian scholars to probe every area of life and thought. Does God exist? What is beauty? How does the mind work? How does the body function? How can diseases be cured? How can technology be created to improve life? Christians have contributions to make in all these fields. Some Christians will specialize in these fields, and other Christians whose gifts and vocations lie in different areas can support them and affirm their roles in the Body, the Church.

Churches can do more to support the idea of loving God with the mind. The Church can become more of a focal point for intellectual life rather than a place where most of the mind is left at the door. In addition to traditional worship services, some churches sponsor lectures, discussions, and classes about issues of the mind that are related to the Christian life. My own church sponsored a six-week Wednesday night series with special lectures and discussions on issues such as Christianity and science, hidden worldviews that undermine faith, top reasons that people dislike Christians, and other topics. We brought in scientists and scholars and invited the whole church into the discussion. Another church sponsored a lecture series I attended in which the pastor and a C. S. Lewis scholar looked at the spiritual implications of the Narnia movies shortly before one of the movies was released. My own pastor sometimes teams with a biblical scholar to do an in-depth study of one of the books of the Bible.

The value of efforts like these is that they not only spark important discussions among church members but also fire the imaginations of individual Christians in ways that may help them spiritually. Many Christians who don't think the intellectual life has much to offer them change their minds when they come across just the right book that inspires them and moves them to a closer relationship with God. Ideas can be as thrilling as any awe-inspiring view from the top of a mountain or soaring melody from a brilliant composer. I vividly recall late nights in college when I stayed up long after my roommates had gone to bed so that I could read Lewis's *Mere Christianity*. The book gripped me so hard I couldn't sit still. I read for a while and then paced the room and listened to music on the headphones and then read some more.

One night one of my roommates came out of his bedroom and asked me to quiet down because I had woken him up with "that noise" I was making. What noise? Apparently

GOD IN THE ORDINARY

I was singing out loud occasionally as the music streamed through my headphones and Lewis's ideas stabbed through my soul. I couldn't help it. It was all I could do to keep from waking up the whole apartment and dragging them into the living room to let me read the book to them. Years later I read *Dark Night of the Soul* by St. John of the Cross and also felt as if someone had drilled down to the core of my mind. I believe God's presence met me in those intense times.

Loving God with the mind is not reserved only for intellectuals. All of us can choose to use our minds to rigorously seek the truth and love God more deeply.

Some Closing Thoughts on God in the Ordinary

God inhabits the ordinary. So far these chapters have explored how God's presence permeates music, nature, the intellect, Scripture, prayer, science, astronomy, relationships, and other areas of life, if only we are awake to Him. That list is only a starting point. Maybe as you read this you can think of many other areas of ordinary life that God's Spirit invades. What about your calling or vocation? Do you sense God's presence as you fulfill the work He has given you to do? We've seen the ways God inhabits music, but what about other art forms? Could this human drive to imagine and create new worlds in novels, paintings, and films be a kind of longing for heaven, the world we haven't yet seen but toward which our affections are pulled? Revelation describes the New Jerusalem as a city with many gates. Are those gates an indication that in heaven we'll spend much of our time traveling back and forth from home, perhaps to distant planets across the universe? Is it possible that one reason we enjoy movies so much is that they are a foretaste of this travel, zipping us from place to place in seconds, transporting us to worlds far beyond what we've ever known ourselves?

109

Where else have you known God's presence? Have you sensed Him even in your suffering, or perhaps *especially* in your suffering, when the trivialities of life are swept away and you are forced to focus only on the things that matter most? In those dark times, have you known the peace that passes understanding as the Holy Spirit comes powerfully and lovingly near even though the suffering itself doesn't stop?

Have you sensed God's Spirit in the sacraments of the Church, such as baptism and Communion, which are so common that it's easy to glide right through them without giving much thought to how they connect us to God? Barbara Brown Taylor points out that "God speaks the language of the flesh" in the sense that many of these sacraments are built on the everyday elements of life—water, wine, bread. She writes,

> Why else did Jesus spend his last night on earth teaching his disciples to wash feet and share supper? With all the conceptual truths of the universe at his disposal, he did not give them something to think about together when he was gone. Instead, he gave them concrete things to do—specific ways of being together in their bodies—that would go on teaching them what they needed to know when he was no longer around to teach them himself."[5]

Jesus is so down to earth, so *connected* to earth in His teaching, that it seems hard to imagine that anyone would miss the meaning, yet people miss it all the time. They don't have "ears to hear." They are not awake to His message, but not because it isn't tied to the ordinary ingredients of life. In his book *God Hides in Plain Sight* Dean Nelson writes,

> It is no coincidence that Jesus called himself the Bread of Life and that he told the woman at the well that he

could provide her with water that will quench her thirst. It's no coincidence that he changed the nature of the wedding at Cana by turning water into wine, and that he fed five thousand with one basket of bread and fish.[6]

One of my favorite representations of people waking up to the beauty of their ordinary lives is in Thornton Wilder's play *Our Town*. In it one of the characters has died as a young woman and is allowed to go back and relive one of her favorite days. Emily chooses her twelfth birthday. She is allowed not only to live the day but also to *see* herself living it. As she goes to the town as it was fourteen years earlier and walks into her mother's kitchen, every simple detail sparkles with significance for her. As Emily becomes her twelve-year-old self, she longs for her mother to stop and truly look at her. But her mother is bustling around, not really aware of her own life. She's asleep to it, as Emily finally realizes most people are. She asks the Stage Manager, who acts as the narrator of the play, "Do any human beings ever realize life while they live it?—every, every minute?" They don't, he says, except maybe a few saints and poets.

Remaining in the midst of the beauty she had so long taken for granted is too painful for Emily, so she quickly ends her visit to the past, saying, "Good-bye to clocks ticking—and Mama's sunflowers. And food and coffee. And new-ironed dresses and hot baths—and sleeping and waking up. Oh, earth, you're too wonderful for anybody to realize you."[7]

I recently attended a performance of this play, and the next morning my own twelve-year-old daughter asked me to help her clean out and rearrange her bedroom. This was a rare impulse for her. She usually wanted to hold on to her old toys and not throw anything away even if she hadn't used it for ages, but suddenly she decided it was time to get rid of the clutter of her childhood and create more space. One of the boxes we sifted through contained some of her own baby clothes that she had later used for her dolls. As she lifted up a little dress or hat or bib, bright memories flashed through my mind of the days when Katie wore them herself. She felt no attachment to them now and threw them into the discard pile as soon as she held them up, but I picked them up again and looked and remembered. I tried to tell Katie my memories of her tumbling around in those outfits, but she wasn't too interested—she had work to do.

With *Our Town* still in my mind, I thought how much I would give to be able to repeat one afternoon when Katie was tiny enough to fit into those dresses. To be able to pick her up and spin her around and hear that little voice, and to have her brother barge in and jump on my back or take hold of my leg to try to pull me down—what would that be worth? Yet when they *were* that age, especially when I was alone with them when Jacob was two and Katie was one and my wife worked long weekend hours at the hospital, the days sometimes seemed like endurance tests of diaper changes, fussiness, bottles, messes, and constant demands. I often couldn't wait for the day to pass so my wife could get home to help me or the kids could finally go to sleep and we could have some adult time. I loved my kids and was intermittently aware of how fortunate we were to have them, but much of the time I was simply trying to get through the day and was glad when it ended.

I am much the same way when it comes to God's presence. I am intermittently aware of Him, but much of the time I'm really not paying attention. There are moments when I sense Him moving in close. In those times I not only have faith that He loves me, but I feel it, too, and I sense that I am headed somewhere and that life here is only the beginning. Those moments always fade, and I'm back to simply slogging through the day. Part of that is simply the distractions of life, but is something more at work? Is there a natural ebb and flow to our awareness of God's presence that is built into the ways He chooses to relate to us? That is the subject of the next chapter.

Go to beaconhillbooks.com for a free downloadable study guide that includes questions for deeper personal reflection as well as activities for use in a small-group setting.

eight ☒ ☒ ☒
GOD CONCEALING, GOD REVEALING

■ Is God close, or is He distant? Or is He somehow both at the same time?

In my own Christian life I have reluctantly come to accept the fact that I can't hold on to my awareness of God's presence all the time. I have had many powerful spiritual moments in which I have felt the loving Holy Spirit hovering all around me. Those moments always fade, and then I am caught up again in the world's static.

When I was a teenager and a very enthusiastic young Christian, I used to feel guilty about these times of my waning awareness of God. If I would spend a week, for instance, at one of the inspiring teen camps our church sponsored, I would come home brimming with joy from having been immersed in daily worship with fellow believers, study of Scripture, teaching from good speakers, fun in the lakes and woods, and prayer alone and with friends. The boundary between me and the heavenly world felt thin. God was close.

I could never sustain those spiritual high points forever, and I don't know anyone who can, but I used to think that if only I had stronger faith, I would get to the point where I *would* be constantly aware of God's presence and would live every day in that joy I had known. I no longer think that. As earlier chapters have shown, one problem with sustaining a spiritual focus is that the world throws endless distractions at us. It's hard these days to keep a constant focus on anything. Even in a less chaotic world, human beings have a natural ebb and flow of concentration and awareness.

But I believe something else is going on also, which I didn't give much thought as a teenager. I believe God also reveals and conceals His Spirit, according to His own purposes. He is always with us, I believe, but He does not always make himself known in obvious ways. When our sense of Him is less acute than it was at a spiritual high point, that doesn't necessarily signal that our faith is waning. I used to put so much emphasis on what *I* was doing in my relationship with God that I overlooked that God may have His own reasons for making my awareness of Him stronger at some times than at others.

Does God hold back? Understandably, the emphasis of much of Christian teaching is that God is reaching out toward us and wanting to draw us close. He made a way for our salvation through Jesus Christ precisely to bridge the spiritual chasm that kept us apart. Thank God that is true. I am drawn to portions of the Bible that emphasize the closeness between us and God. I love John 15, when Jesus tells His disciples, "As the Father has loved me, so have I loved you. Now remain in my love" (John 15:9), and later in that chapter, "I no longer call you servants, because a servant does not know his master's business. Instead, I have called you friends, for everything that I learned from my Father I have made known to you" (John 15:15). I could read Romans 8 again and again, especially the verses that say things like

"The Spirit you received does not make you slaves, so that you live in fear again; rather, the Spirit you received brought about your adoption to sonship. And by him we cry, 'Abba, Father.' The Spirit himself testifies with our spirit that we are God's children" (Romans 8:15-16).

I relish verses like this that describe God's intimacy, but that is not the only way God is portrayed in the Bible, nor is it the only way the life of faith is shown. As a Christian I long for the breakthrough moments when God's presence is bright and unmistakable. I would love for Him to appear in such a blaze of power that I am awestruck and knocked to my knees.

I want an event like the Mount of Transfiguration recorded in the Gospels. Imagine yourself on top of that mountain with Jesus. When He prays, His clothes suddenly become as bright as a flash of lightning. Witnessing that alone would be thrilling, but then two of the greatest figures of the Old Testament, Moses and Elijah, two men of history who should be long dead but who are very much alive, appear with Jesus in glorious splendor and start a conversation among the three of them. It gets even more dramatic. A bright cloud appears and envelops them, and then the voice of God himself says from the cloud, "This is my Son, whom I love. Listen to him!" (Mark 9:7).

This leaves Peter sputtering. He wants to build three shelters, one for Jesus, one for Moses, one for Elijah. Luke's account of this scene says bluntly, "He did not know what he was saying" (Luke 9:33). But I understand his impulse. A tremendous event is taking place. A moment like this makes it worth becoming a disciple. Peter wants to hang on to it somehow. "It is good for us to be here," he says. The boundary between the mundane world and the spiritual world beyond has been torn away, and the two have come together on that mountain. Peter wants to make it last.

It doesn't last. Once the voice speaks, Peter and the others look over to see that Moses and Elijah are no longer there. Jesus stands alone. No more dazzling clothes, no more bright cloud, no voice from heaven. Already the demands of harsh reality are urging them back down the mountain. Can they at least go tell everyone this story and live in the afterglow of this memory for a while? No, Jesus tells them not to say a word to anyone about it until after He has been raised from the dead.

At the bottom of that mountain they find only trouble. A man with an epileptic son comes and complains that Jesus' disciples, the ones who didn't even get to see the Transfiguration, had been unable to heal the boy. "'You unbelieving and perverse generation,' Jesus replied, 'how long shall I stay with you? How long shall I put up with you? Bring the boy here to me'" (Matthew 17:17). Jesus heals him, but this tense encounter, filled with Jesus' disappointment in His disciples, is a huge let-down from the ecstatic scene that had taken place such a short time before. How could the glorious moment fade so quickly?

I have known this same kind of deflating letdown in my own life of faith. When I sense His presence in a powerful, ecstatic moment, I realize that He is all I want and need. I will cling to this intense awareness of Him forever. I won't let it fade.

But then I drift off into the deadened reality of everyday life, with its cloud of unbelief. I don't lose my faith, but the ecstasy fades. If I make the mistake of equating my faith with that feeling, then I might wrongly conclude that the fading of the elation means a diminishment of my commitment or connection to Christ. Some do walk away from their faith during these times of deadened emotions, assuming it must not have been true to begin with.

Miracles Are Not What Faith Is Made Of

Jesus tries to keep His disciples from tying their faith to these emotional high points. He could have arranged a Transfiguration every day if He had wanted to. He doesn't. It happens only once, and even then He downplays it. Only a few of the disciples get to see it, and certainly not the public at large. Even the few who do get to see it aren't allowed to talk about it until much later. Once the event is over, Jesus takes His disciples right back to the tough business at hand. There's work to be done. The transcendent moment is important. Peter was right to say that "it is good for us to be here," but you can't live on that mountain. The people are down below.

Miracles and deeply emotional encounters with God's presence have their place in the Christian life. I would dread a faith that was cut off from the deep sense of joy that comes from feeling the Holy Spirit hovering in music or nature or prayer or in times of distress. Jesus doesn't try to cut off His followers from those feelings or from spectacular events, but He knows those things aren't what sustain long-lasting faith.

Even though it may seem as if you could never doubt Jesus or want to walk away from Him once you had experienced something as amazing as the Transfiguration, the same Peter who witnessed that event also denied Jesus multiple times not long afterwards, once Jesus was under arrest and the promising days appeared to be over and all Peter's dreams were shattered. "I don't know Him," Peter says. If the miracles that Peter saw were not enough to guarantee that his faith never faltered, then what chance do the rest of us stand of building a solid spiritual foundation on emotion or spectacle, since we have much less of it?

Peter's denial of Jesus was not the end of the story. He was restored and went on to become a mighty leader of the Church. His spiritual failure had not been inevitable. Many people hang on to their faith regardless of circumstances or feelings. But even though failure is not inevitable, the fluctuation in our awareness of God is. Belief fades in and out. That's the nature of it. Better to learn that during times our faith is strong so that when feelings fade or belief falters, we can still hang on to the *knowledge* of God's presence. A doubt doesn't need to alarm us or wreck our faith.

The greatest spiritual heroes have wavered in their belief. Peter is one example, and John the Baptist is another. Think of what John witnessed. He not only saw Jesus in person but also baptized Him. As He did so, the heavens opened up and the Holy Spirit descended like a dove, and the very voice of God said, "This is my Son, whom I love; with him I am well pleased" (Matthew 3:17). What more confirmation of your faith could you possibly ask for than to hear and see the Father, Son, and Holy Spirit at the same time in the same place? It was one of the most extraordinary spiritual moments in history. If you had been there to see it for yourself, would it have been enough to sustain your faith for a lifetime? You might think so, but even for a giant of the faith like John the Baptist, the moment faded. Once he was in prison not too long after that, he began wondering. He sent his disciples to Jesus to ask, "Are you the one who was to come, or should we expect someone else?" (Matthew 11:3).

Expect someone else? Are you kidding? What more could John expect than what he had already seen? Jesus would have been justified in giving John a harsh answer to this question. He might have said, "Well, John, if you're not yet convinced about me after all you have witnessed, then I give up. I don't know what else it will take."

Instead, Jesus gives an answer that is kind and uplifting: "Go back and report to John what you hear and see: The blind receive sight, the lame walk, those who have leprosy are cured, the deaf hear, the dead are raised, and the good news is preached to the poor. Blessed is anyone who does not stumble on account of me" (Matthew 11:4-6). Jesus knew that big moments fade. Faith must be constantly renewed. He focused not on amazing events of the past but rather on what He was doing *right now* to build the kingdom of God. He knew that if John heard that, it would be enough to sustain his faith while he endured the torment of prison.

Jesus had ruled out spectacle or emotion as ways to sustain faith even before His public ministry began. During His forty days of temptation in the desert, the devil took Him to stand on the highest point of the Temple. "'If you are the Son of God,' he said, 'throw yourself down. For it is written: "He will command his angels concerning you, and they will lift you up in their hands, so that you will not strike your foot against a stone"'" (Matthew 4:6). Tim Stafford writes about this temptation, "What Jesus stands to gain from such a stunt is unclear. Will the miracle make a PR splash? Will it jumpstart his attempt to bring God's kingdom to life? Alternatively, will such a miracle overcome any of Jesus' own lingering questions and reassure him once and for all that God is fully on his side?"[1]

Jesus never finds out what the result of such a leap would be, because He rejects the temptation. He does so with a verse of Scripture: "Do not put the Lord your God to the test" (Matthew 4:7). God will not be manipulated into proving himself to us. He won't be backed into a corner to prove He is real or to prove He is with us or that He loves us or that He will pull us through. Sometimes He will act so dramatically and hover close to us so lovingly that we will be left stunned and inspired. Other times He won't seem to be there at all. We can't conjure Him up or force His hand. He is God. Part of faith is trusting that He is there even in the most silent, lonely moments. Jesus had no intention of building His ministry on stunts or emotional manipulation, either of the Heavenly Father or His own followers. The devil couldn't make Him jump from the Temple or do any other tricks. Neither can we.

Why God Can Be Scary

I so long for God's presence that it's easy to forget that in much of Scripture, especially in the Old Testament, people often wanted just the opposite. Even though they were God's followers, they were *afraid* of His presence because His power and holiness could kill them. As fallen people in a sinful world, we know that a wide gulf separates us from God. Salvation through Jesus Christ, if we accept it, ultimately bridges that gulf. But God's holiness in the face of sin is not to be taken lightly.

For Christians, who rely on Jesus Christ for salvation and the Holy Spirit for guidance, the ebb and flow of our sense of God's presence is an internal, spiritual matter. In the Old Testament, with the Israelites who relied on God to achieve freedom from Pharaoh and then inched their way across the desert toward the Promised Land, God's presence was physical. They had to be careful how and when they came into contact with that presence. God revealed and concealed himself in ways that may help us better understand how He moves in our own lives in a much different era.

In Exodus God's physical presence was dangerous. He was holy and mighty, and the sinful people He was guiding across the desert could not approach Him casually. Elaborate precautions were put into place to keep people from getting so close that they would be destroyed. Before Moses went up Mount Sinai to receive the Ten Commandments, repeated warnings were given for the people not to get too close. God didn't keep them away completely. He could have done so, but He chose to let them hear and see Him—within limits. They had to stay at the foot of the mountain beyond a certain boundary. The Lord told Moses, "Put limits for the people around the mountain and tell them, 'Be careful that you do not approach the mountain or touch the foot of it. Whoever touches the mountain is to be put to death'" (Exodus 19:12). Several other warnings are given in these chapters with the same message: keep your distance.

Yet God did appear. He descended in fire, and the mountain was bathed in smoke. "The smoke billowed up from it like smoke from a furnace, and the whole mountain trembled violently [and] the sound of the trumpet grew louder and louder" (Exodus 19:18-19). Despite the gulf that exists between a holy God and a sinful people, God was reaching out to them. He allowed their spokesman, Moses, to go all the way up the mountain. In fact, solidifying Moses' leadership was a key reason for the dramatic scene they were allowed to witness. The Lord said, "I am going to come to you in a dense cloud, so that the people will hear me speaking with you and will always put their trust in you" (Exodus 19:9). The spectacle of the smoke and fire and trembling and thunder and lightning and trumpet blasts on the mountain was one way God revealed himself to the people, and the words Moses brought down the mountain were another way.

Even with Moses, who gets closer to the Lord than anyone else in Exodus, God reveals and conceals. Exodus 33 is a fascinating illustration of this. It begins just after the outrageous incident in which the people betrayed God by urging Aaron to make the golden calf for them to worship after Moses had been away so long on Mount Sinai. Moses goes to the Lord to plead for forgiveness. God tells Moses to take the people away from the place where they are camped and head toward the Promised Land. God says He will send an angel to drive out their enemies. And then He says these ominous words: "But I will not go with you, because you are a stiff-necked people and I might destroy you on the way" (Exodus 33:3). God's holiness, a concept hard to fully appreciate in our own irreverent day, is incompatible with the brazen sin of the people. God pulls away.

Moses, however, sets up a "tent of meeting" outside the camp, and the pillar of cloud, in which God's presence dwells, stands at the tent and speaks to Moses "as one speaks to a friend" (Exodus 33:11). The people look on from a distance. Moses seeks reassurance, and he wants God's presence to go with them on the journey. God answers his plea. "My Presence will go with you, and I will give you rest" (verse 14). Moses doesn't want to continue under any other circumstances. "If your Presence does not go with us," he says, "do not send us up from here" (verse 15). The Lord shows His profound closeness to Moses by saying, "I will do the very thing you have asked, because I am pleased with you and I know you by name" (Exodus 33:17).

Those are extraordinary words for the Lord to speak. So far the thrust of the scene seems to be more about revealing than concealing. But as God speaks (*outside* the camp, to Moses but not the people), He is wrapped in a cloud. Even in a moment of amazing closeness, God is still also hidden. Scripture says nothing about Moses' feelings during all this, and I cannot fathom what they must have been. How thrilling and deeply moving it must have been to have talked to God so directly! Yet perhaps the closeness makes Moses want to sweep away all the remaining barriers between Him and God, because He goes one step further by asking, "Now show me your glory." Biblical scholar Robert Alter writes that "We are not likely to recover precisely what the key term *kavod*—glory, honor, divine presence, and very literally, 'weightiness'—conveyed to the ancient Hebrew imagination."[2] What is clear is that Moses wanted to know God more. Have you ever been so close to God's presence that it made you only want to press in further?

Once again, God answers by revealing and concealing:

Revealing: "I will cause all my goodness to pass in front of you, and I will proclaim my name, the LORD, in your presence" (Exodus 33:19).

Concealing: "You cannot see my face, for no one may see me and live" (Exodus 33:20).

Revealing and concealing: "When my glory passes by, I will put you in a cleft in the rock and cover you with my hand until I have passed by. Then I will remove my hand and you will see my back; but my face must not be seen" (Exodus 33:22-23).

Only Moses came so close to God, but even for him, was it enough? Did it satisfy his desire to know God fully? And what about everyone else, who could only look on at a distance as they stood at the entrance of their tents and gazed at the pillar of cloud that stood before Moses? Did they long to draw closer to God for themselves?

God in Smoke, God in Fire: The Tabernacle Reveals and Conceals

For modern readers, the pacing of the Book of Exodus is strange. The story is dramatic, but the action parts sometimes grind to a halt as long lists of instructions or laws are given. One of those times is when the thrilling story of God's glory appearing as a consuming fire on top of the mountain is followed by seven chapters giving a long list of minute details about the Tabernacle that is to be built and all the accouterments that are to go with it. Why so much detail about measurements and garments and fabrics and furniture at that point in the book? Alter points out that in contrast to the people's "fearful distance from the fiery divine presence" on the mountain, the "architectural plan for the Tabernacle and its decor offers a reassuring antithesis. God will come down from above to dwell among His people within the securely designated sanctum of the Tabernacle."[3] During the time when the people are most afraid, God is already making a way to place His presence in the midst of them.

Is the Tabernacle designed to reveal God or conceal Him? In one sense, it reveals Him more vividly than anything we have today. His very presence hovered in physical form over the Tabernacle day and night. It looked like a pillar of cloud during the day and fire at night. The people could see it not only with eyes of faith, as we see God, but also with their physical eyes. When the pillar lifted from the Tabernacle, it was time for the people to pack up and move forward, with God's presence in the pillar to lead them. That is a physical manifestation of God that many of us would welcome. They could *see* Him there and follow Him when He moved.

On the other hand, the Tabernacle was designed in a way that kept God at a distance. Although it was a kind of elaborate portable tent, people could not walk in and out of it at will. They could see the pillar hovering over it, concealed in cloud, but they could not go in to the center of the Tabernacle, the most holy place or holy of holies, to see where the Shekinah, the visible manifestation of God's Spirit, was enthroned on the ark of the covenant. Only the high priest could go all the way in, and even he could go there only once a year, to sprinkle the blood that would atone for the sins of the people.

The very design of the Tabernacle kept God's presence concealed. The Tabernacle did not open directly onto the encampment where the people stayed. It opened onto a courtyard, where priests offered animal sacrifices at the altar and other aspects of worship took place. Throughout this book I have spoken in spiritual terms of a boundary, or veil, that separates us from the eternal realm. The Tabernacle had *literal* veils—levels of concealment—that separated the people from God. Priests would enter the Tabernacle through the outer veil and go into the room that contained the showbread, the seven-branched golden candlestick, and golden altar with its incense. Beyond that room, through a second veil, was the innermost holy place. When the high priest entered it once a year, he went in only after careful preparation and wearing elaborate garments in which every detail carried symbolic significance.

Even for the high priest, entering into God's presence had to be done with the utmost care. Bells were sewn onto the hem of his robe. As Exodus 28:35 says, "The sound of the bells will be heard when he enters the Holy Place before the LORD and when he comes out, so that he will not die." Alter explains that "the inner sanctum was a dangerous place. Any misstep or involuntary trespass of the sacred paraphernalia could bring death."[4] Some commentators believe the bells were there to indicate whether or not the priest was still alive.

On the physical level, these rituals and garments and veils have been swept aside, replaced by what they foreshadowed, the sacrifice of Jesus Christ to cover our sins. But

I like to ponder these methods God used to interact with the people, because they *were* so physical. I understand God in the cloud. That's exactly how He seems to me, close enough to see and revere in one sense and yet shrouded in mystery at the same time. I can relate to the close-yet-remote God on that burning, smoking mountain. I would have been right on the edge of that boundary, straining to see as much as I could. I understand the frustration of the Israelites at the base of Mount Sinai as they waited for Moses to come down, wondering what must have gone wrong. *Why was he taking so long?* The trembling of the mountain and smoke and fire were long gone—*would those spectacles ever return? Had Moses abandoned his people? Had God abandoned them too?*

It's easy to read the story now and see that neither God nor Moses had abandoned them. Magnificent work was being done on the Israelites' behalf on top of that mountain, but they couldn't *see* it. They were left in the dark about so much of God's plans and purposes, as we still are today. We see in part. We see enough to keep us going, to keep us hanging on to the Lord.

We live in shadow and foreshadow. Instead of a high priest entering the Most Holy Place through veils to sprinkle the blood of animals, we have Jesus Christ as our high priest, entering "the most holy place once for all by his own blood, thus obtaining eternal redemption," as Hebrews 9:12 says. The great "faith chapter" of Hebrews 11 gives a long and inspiring list of people in biblical history who "did not receive the things promised; they only saw them and welcomed them from a distance" (Hebrews 11:13). These people, such as Abraham, Sarah, Noah, Enoch, Jacob, Rahab, Gideon, and many others "were longing for a better country—a heavenly one" (Hebrews 11:16). They lived by faith, which the Hebrews author defines as "confidence in what we hope for and assurance about what we do not see" (Hebrews 11:1).

I believe the obstructions that keep God in shadow and smoke and mystery will soon be cleared away as this earth passes away and is replaced by the new heaven and earth for eternity. As Revelation 21:3 says, "Look! God's dwelling place is now among the people, and he will dwell with them. They will be his people, and God himself will be with them and be their God. He will wipe every tear from their eyes. There will be no more death or mourning or crying or pain, for the old order of things has passed away." God will live with His people—no mention of veils or barriers anymore.

The Gravitational Pull Toward God

I was moved by the story in *Christianity Today* of Frank A. James III, whose brother died on Mount Hood when he was trapped in a blizzard that prevented rescuers from reaching him until it was too late. The grief over this loss was the worst pain James had ever known. Though he is a preacher and seminary provost, he said he "found it agonizingly difficult to come to terms with my brother's death." One question still haunts him: "Where was God when Kelly was freezing to death on Mount Hood?"

James has searched for an answer but has not found one. "So where was God? I don't know. I may never know." He cannot explain God's distance, but it has had a much different effect on his faith than he expected. Although intense grief and disappointment sometimes lead to bitterness, that has not happened for James. "There is disappointment, sadness, and confusion, but oddly, there is no retreat from God. Instead, I find myself drawn to God. To be sure, he is more enigmatic than I thought, but I still can't shake loose from him. There seems to be a kind of gravitational pull toward God."[5]

A "gravitational pull toward God"—I know exactly what he means. You can see it in any of the psalms of lament—a desperate crying out to God because of His absence or distance, followed by—in the end—the certainty that He will return and prevail. Psalm 69, for instance, begins with the agonizing plea "Save me, O God, for the waters have come up to my neck. I sink in the miry depths, where there is no foothold. . . . I am worn out calling for help; my throat is parched. My eyes fail, looking for my God" (69:1-3). The writer is in despair over God's hiddenness, but he still can't get away from Him or the faith that He has not abandoned His people. Some of the later verses say, "The LORD hears the needy and does not despise his captive people. Let heaven and earth praise him, the seas and all that move in them, for God will save Zion and rebuild the cities of Judah" (69:33-35).

I have been a Christian since I was eight years old, but when I think of the time when I came closest to turning away from Christ, I recall a dark period when I was a freshman in college. I was besieged by doubt, confusion, and temptation. God felt more distant than ever. More than ever before, I questioned whether He was really there. I drifted from Him for a while and then purposely pushed my faith aside. I tried to reason and rationalize my faith out of my life. Eventually I could no longer accept the inner turmoil of calling myself a Christian while inwardly pushing God away. I had to come to a decision.

One night I found myself alone in my dorm room. I remember the moment vividly. I sat at my desk and thought, the life I'm leading is dishonest. If I'm no longer a believer, shouldn't I admit it, at least to myself? I stared into space for a long time before I finally worked up the courage to declare, *I am no longer a Christian.*

And that's when something strange happened, a story I have kept to myself because it's so hard to explain and so different from almost all the rest of my Christian life. In the moment my mind formed that thought that I was no longer a Christian, the Holy Spirit swept over me more powerfully than I have ever experienced before or since. I felt the sensation of arms wrapping around me as wave after wave of what I can only describe as forgiveness washed over me. I leaned forward, barely able to contain the onslaught. I heard no audible voice, but the words I heard the Holy Spirit impressing on my mind were these: *I will not let you go.*

I can't explain what happened that day. Why would God wait until I was ready to take my final step away from Him before He swooped in? Why would He cover me with forgiveness when I wasn't seeking it? God's gravitational pull was drawing me back to Him. I could have pulled away again, but I no longer wanted to. My faith was powerfully restored that day, and from that day to this, through doubts, joys, failings, and triumphs, I have never walked away from Him again.

Sometimes the veil between us and God's presence is thick, maybe impenetrable. If we know to expect these times, then it's easier to bear them until the cloud that obscures Him dissipates. One danger we face when His Spirit seems far away is settling for a counterfeit. That danger is the subject of the next chapter.

Go to beaconhillbooks.com for a free downloadable study guide that includes questions for deeper personal reflection as well as activities for use in a small-group setting.

nine ☒ ☒ ☒
THE LURE OF COUNTERFEITS

■ Earlier this summer, out of frustration I complained to my kids that nothing ever seems to be enough for them. No matter how much we give them, no matter how much we spend on the birthday parties or gifts or trips or other things they want, they still don't quite seem satisfied. They have already moved on to the next request, the next thing or experience they just "have" to get in order to make life bearable.

My complaint, common to many parents, is in some ways an exaggeration. Our kids do sometimes show gratitude for what we do for them, but there is some truth in my protest also. My kids are coming to terms with the nagging reality that most of us sense—which is that nothing we have or achieve or are given is enough. We can learn contentment. We can practice gratitude. But I'm talking about something beyond that, the idea that nothing quite lives up to what we think it will do for us. It's tempting to think, *If only I had that house, or that career, or that relationship, or those looks, or that fame, or that set of circumstances, that would be enough. I would be happy. I wouldn't ask for anything more.*

It doesn't work. It's a lie, but many of us can never quite stop believing it. I *know* that money can't buy happiness, and neither can fame or good looks, but when I read an article recently about a handsome, successful, and wealthy young actor who had attempted suicide, my first thought was *Why would he do that? He has everything!* I know only the vaguest details about this man's life, and I know better than to think that looks and money equal happiness, but that lie is so strong that it is still the first thought that pops into my head.

Many people don't achieve that one thing that they believe would bring happiness, so they go through life believing their vague discontent is a result of their failure to grasp that prize. Even if they do get it, they soon realize that as enjoyable and temporarily affirming that thing may be, it still leaves them wanting more.

The pleasures and achievements of this life are fleeting. Even as we are grasping them, they are slipping away from us. "What is your life?" James asks in Scripture. "You are a mist that appears for a little while and then vanishes" (James 5:14). Jesus also warned of the futility of chasing things that look shiny and magnificent but that will soon rot away: "Do not store up for yourselves treasures on earth, where moth and vermin destroy, and where thieves break in and steal" (Matthew 6:19).

What if this longing for some temporary aspiration—a certain career success or romantic relationship or thrilling experience or treasured possession—is really a disguised longing for something bigger? What if it is pointing not to that thing I think I want but to something much more significant and long-lasting? What if it is a longing for eternity built into my soul? Romans 8:22 tells us that not only individuals but also the entirety of creation "has been groaning as in the pains of childbirth right up to the present time." This longing is not in vain. It will be fulfilled, but not by the temporary objects of desire. Paul writes, "I consider that our present sufferings are not worth comparing with the glory that will be revealed in us" (Romans 8:18).

If all this longing is a disguised hope for the eternal, then many of the good things that are sprinkled through our lives—and toward which we feel such affection—may be seen as *foretastes* of that eternity. Music, nature, beauty, literature, physical adventure, good food, the intellect, homes, relationships, fun, the experience of God's loving presence—all of these are part of the eternal life that awaits the redeemed in Christ who live in eternity with God.

The problem is that if these things are a *foretaste* of what is to come, that means they're a *hint* of it. They're not the real thing, or at least not *all* of the real thing. Everything toward which we are headed is better. The heaven in which we will spend eternity is a place in which longings *are* finally fulfilled. No more false promises of "If only I had that one thing" followed by vague disappointment even if I get it. It is a hope worth dwelling on. And yet it's a hope that can also feel too distant. In the scheme of things, of course, it isn't very far away. An entire lifetime is no more than a puff of air in the span of eternity. On the other hand, a really bad hour can *feel* like eternity.

As I write this, I'm scheduled for an upcoming surgery that is not life-threatening but will be inconvenient and painful and will leave my face bandaged and scarred for quite some time. I'm dreading it. I've had other such surgeries, and I know that in the long run I heal and am ultimately better off. But right now it looms large, certainly larger in my mind than the promise of anything that may happen a year from now, or ten years, or in eternity. It's hard to think with much clarity about six months from now, let alone eternity. The thought of a bright eternal future is tantalizing but also hard to grasp, and less emotionally gripping than the challenges of getting through the next month.

Faced with the elusive nature of the things that bring *real* fulfillment, my temptation is to grab what I can get *now*, even if it's a counterfeit, and often even if it's ultimately disappointing or destructive.

The Seduction of the Dazzling Counterfeit God

What will bring fulfillment, love, salvation? What provides authentic joy? Who or what is worthy of adoration? Where is real community? What is true? What will satisfy?

People seek answers to those questions every day, even when they're not consciously aware that they're asking them. Christians believe all these things are found in Jesus Christ. If so, then why would anyone, sometimes including Christians themselves, settle for counterfeit gods?

The false gods offer the ease and satisfaction of immediate gratification. Serving the true God requires the rigors of commitment, faith, the slow unfolding of a plan whose fulfillment may not be clear until eternity. What are these counterfeits? Some are big and obvious and can completely consume someone's life. Almost anything, for instance, that can have the word "addiction" following it qualifies as a counterfeit—drug addiction, alcohol addiction, sex addiction, Internet addiction, work addiction. Some Christians believe themselves immune from counterfeits if they are not ensnared by these easily identifiable ones. They may not struggle with much of a temptation toward things like drugs or alcohol. They love the Lord and assume that nothing else in their lives would ever be powerful enough to rival their devotion to Him.

The problem with counterfeit gods is that they are as sneaky as counterfeits of anything else, such as money or art. The counterfeit doesn't announce itself. The whole idea of a counterfeit is to make a person encountering it think, *This is the real thing. This is what you're looking for. You don't need to be on guard against this.*

To *some* degree, the counterfeit *is* real. Think of a counterfeit painting or a fake twenty-dollar bill. It shares many of the same qualities of the real thing. It's not just that it *looks* real, but it actually possesses many of the same real traits. A counterfeit painting can be just as beautiful as the real thing. An undetected counterfeit bill can buy the same items as a real one. But the owners of these counterfeits don't have what they think they have. They have been lied to. They have been fooled.

It's similar with counterfeit gods. They have their appeal, but big lies are embedded in their core. One lie is the idea that because the counterfeit has good elements in it, my intense devotion to it will not be a problem. Take materialism, one of the most pervasive of the counterfeit gods. Everybody needs food and shelter and clothing to live. To own something is not to serve it as a god. Part of what we do as Christians is to give to the poor so they can have these necessities. Buying and selling keep economies robust and people employed. Working hard and reaping the material rewards of that labor bring dignity and satisfaction. Christians thank God when they have good jobs and the ability to support those who depend on them and to support their church and enjoy the world He has given.

But money can easily sneak in and become a counterfeit god. It almost always sneaks. I personally don't know anyone who would actually say, *I worship money.* Everyone knows money can't bring happiness, but few really *believe* it. At the intellectual level, it's easy to look around and see countless examples of wealth that has not brought lasting fulfillment or salvation. But at a deeper, unspoken level of desire, it's easy to believe, *If only I had a little more, I would be satisfied.* Many who fall under the spell of this counterfeit god don't fall in love with money in general, but rather they put their hope in one object or one vision of what money can bring them. *If only I had that house,* they think, or *If only I had that car, I would be the person I was meant to be.* If they ever articulated the desire that bluntly, the falsity of the idea might be easy to identify, but these desires are rarely brought out into the open.

Finding the House That Would Make Me a Better Man

Let me illustrate the allure of the counterfeit with two stories of finding the perfect house. The first has to do with a little fantasy I enact each Sunday as I read the *Los Angeles Times.* Every week the real estate section of that newspaper runs a "Home of the Week" feature. It gives a description and runs several photographs of a beautiful house, almost always costing multi-millions, that has just gone on the market. The pictures show perfect lawns, sometimes patios overlooking the ocean, sprawling living rooms tastefully decorated and without a spot of clutter. I read these stories each week and picture myself in those homes. How content I would be in such a place! How successful I would feel! Sophisticated. A master of life's circumstances. I could entertain generously, read deeply, write with a concentration never imagined elsewhere. I would feel more magnanimous toward the world.

My second house fantasy focuses on a house near where I live. When I drive to my children's middle school to pick them up in the afternoons, I park across the street from an ideal house. It's not a mansion but a beautifully preserved older home—blue with white trim, a lawn filled with roses and precisely trimmed bushes, a porch swing hanging on the wide, old-fashioned porch—a house in which to live a tidy, carefree, simple life, swinging on the porch, enjoying the roses, gazing at the mountains in the distance, a house of lemonade and the laughter of neighborhood children.

Both of these house fantasies are harmless daydreams, perhaps, but do you see the lie embedded in them? They invest the house with powers beyond what a house can accomplish. These fantasies make the house not simply a nice structure but also a place that can generate contentment, magnanimity, serenity. The right house can even make *me* better.

Does a house really have that power?

After playing around with the fantasy of the blue house each day while waiting to pick up my kids, I finally dug into it a little deeper one afternoon while I was parked at the curb. I looked at it carefully and wondered, *How satisfying would it* really *be to live there?* How much different would it be from living in the pleasant but modest home I already inhabit, where it's hard to think of anything but all the work that needs done—the fence that needs repaired and the trim painted and the carpets cleaned and the hedges trimmed and the sprinklers fixed? In contrast was this perfect blue house with its sculpted lawn and unchipped paint.

However, if I owned it, as I now imagined myself doing, how many days would it take for the illusion of the house's perfection to wear off? Already I could see brown spots in those precisely trimmed hedges. And though the house was beautiful, it was old. Portions of the porch floor sagged. What upgrades might be needed inside, in the kitchen or plumbing or wiring or bathrooms? Would we really want to live this close to the school, with all the noise and traffic? The homeowner burden began to sink down on me. Nice house, but not the answer to all my problems.

I remember years earlier when it looked as if my wife and I might not get to move into the house we own now, the one that needs all the repairs. The sellers kept dragging their feet, and it looked as if the deal would fall through. We *wanted* that house. We had already begun to picture ourselves in every room of it. We fretted over every detail of the deal. We prayed fervently that it wouldn't fall apart. *If only we can get that house,* we thought, *everything will be all right.*

We did get it. We moved in. I'm still grateful for it. All these years later, the house wraps around me like a comfortable blanket. But the house didn't make everything all right. It solved some problems and created others. It didn't make me a better person, didn't make me less irritable or kinder or more patient. It didn't answer all my longings. It didn't save me.

I have known a number of couples who have bought into the illusion of the house-as-answer-to-discontent. They pour their energy into getting the dream house, and if they manage to do so, they often soon start working on acquiring the next one once that house proves not to be the answer. It has become a counterfeit god, possibly one of many they serve—and it always disappoints.

Serving the "Nearby Gods": Why Choose Only One?

One of the dangers of counterfeit gods is that they don't demand that we worship them exclusively. People can accumulate many, with each pushing the real God farther away. A related danger is that it is often hard to tell when a legitimate pleasure or interest crosses the line into becoming a counterfeit god.

Take video games. Harmless diversion or counterfeit god? It depends. Tom Bissell has written a book called *Extra Lives: Why Video Games Matter*, which both defends and criticizes the games. A devotee—or addict—of the games himself, he acknowledges their similarity to a religion in his opening pages. Describing one type of video game, he writes that its pleasures are "ample, complicated, and intensely private; their potency is difficult to explain, sort of like religion, of which these games become, for many, an aspartame form."[1]

Bissell writes frankly of how video games have taken over his life. Before he gave so much of himself over to them, he had a five-year period in which he wrote about 4,500 manuscript pages of work that was published, including several books and more than fifty articles. Today he says, "I play video games in the morning, play video games in the afternoon, and spend my evenings playing video games. These days, I still manage to write, but the times I am able to do so for more than three sustained hours have the temporal periodicity of comets with near-Earth trajectories."[2] At one point a friend of his who shared his love of video games lured him into snorting cocaine so they could play their favorite video game together for the next thirty hours straight.[3] After that, his addictions to video games and cocaine became intertwined.

Despite all the trouble his devotion to video games brought him, Bissell still maintains they also enriched his life. But like all counterfeit gods, they did not fulfill his hopes for them. "Once I wanted games to show me things I could not see in any other medium. Then I wanted games to tell me a story in a way no other medium can. Then I wanted games to redeem something absent in myself."[4] Games, or any other "aspartame" god, could do none of those things. Redemption is not in them, but the false gods can eat away much of life before a person sees that.

Cultures as well as individuals create counterfeit gods to serve. Look at a culture and ask, To what does it pay homage? Where does it put its treasure? What does it love? One such deity in our own culture might be professional sports. I don't mean to paint sports as sinister. There's nothing wrong with kicking back and enjoying a football game. But look at how our culture has elevated sports. A vast amount of money is spent all over the world to build arenas and stadiums far larger than any church or cathedral. The Super Bowl alone is an international obsession that rivals the celebration of any religious or national holiday. Even churches suspend their services and sponsor parties to make it easier for their members to participate in it.

Leaders of nations across the globe compete to bring sports events such as the Olympics to their countries. Billions of dollars are poured into television rights, advertising, products, and outrageous salaries for athletes. Is it too much to say that professional sports is a god in our culture and in the lives of many individuals?

In Exodus the Hebrews met calamity when they made a golden calf to worship *in addition* to the real God as they partied the night away. Was their golden god anywhere near as beloved as the teams and star athletes are to millions of devoted fans in our day? The jewelry the Hebrews turned over to Aaron to make the calf wasn't evil. Even a sculpture of a calf itself is not wrong if it's intended as a work of art or a decorative piece. It became evil when they made it a god.

Professional sports aren't evil. They can be enjoyable and refreshing. But imagine if people put even a *fraction* of the attention, devotion, resources, love, loyalty, time, and enthusiasm directed toward sports into serving others, or praying, or seeking God in a community of believers. How would the world be different?

Why this compulsion toward making and serving counterfeit gods? Perhaps it's because we were created to be connected to the true God, and if that doesn't happen, we learn to settle for substitutes. As psychiatrist Gerald G. May puts it in his book *Addiction and Grace*, "After twenty years of listening to the yearnings of people's hearts, I am convinced that all human beings have an inborn desire for God. Whether we are consciously religious or not, the desire is our deepest longing and our most precious treasure."[5]

"Nearby gods" is the name Monica Ganas gives to the substitute deities people settle for in place of the real one. She writes, "Here's how it works. Let's assume my longing is for the 'god' of eternal life, but I don't trust the real God to get the job done. Well, then, I will worship the nearby god (for example, fame or physical perfection) so that either my name or my image will endure forever."[6]

Our own gods have advantages that make them more convenient to serve than the real God. They can be shaped to our liking and don't make us look into the depths of our souls and confess what is really there so that it can be rooted out. They are flexible. They are fun. We worship them, but we also control them.

One of the "nearby gods" Ganas analyzes is celebrity culture. Celebrities, she says, "must earn our worship. Ancient peoples fed their idols (as we do with box office receipts) and dressed up their idols (as we do with fashion magazines) when they were happy with them. They also spanked their idols (as we do with gossip magazines) whenever they were unhappy."[7] People who are hungry for spiritual connection will grab it wherever they can find it, often in the *easiest* places where they can find it. Their "worship" of the substitute gods often even looks suspiciously similar to the ways people worship the real God. Think of how similar a rock concert is, for instance, to a church worship service, with the community of believers gathered together to sing and share and raise hands and transcend everyday experience. Ganas writes of the movie theater as the "film cathedral," where people eat their "sacramental popcorn" and gaze at the altar of the screen and piece together the story they are told.

In my own field of literature, I have seen people approach literary works with something very close to the reverence usually reserved for a sacred text, and sometimes literature becomes a substitute for the sacred text. None of this is to criticize concerts, movies, or literature. Most Christians will want to have those good things in their lives, but when they become substitutes for real connection with God, when they become ways to temporarily fill the gap left by God's absence in one's life, then they have become false gods.

Spiritual but Not Religious

Because people have such a deep need for spiritual connection, spiritual experience itself sometimes becomes the counterfeit god. One trend is for people to describe themselves as "spiritual but not religious." CNN reported that this label is now so common that its adherents have created their own acronym for—SBNR—and have gathered together on Facebook and elsewhere. According to a LifeWay Christian Resources survey, seventy-two percent of eighteen- to twenty-nine-year-olds describe themselves as "more spiritual than religious."[8] What does that mean? Barbara Brown Taylor writes that when she hears people describe themselves that way, "It may be the name for a longing—for more meaning, more feeling, more connection, more life. . . . They know there is more to life than what meets the eye. They have drawn close to this 'More' in nature, in love, in art, in grief."[9]

Although the "spiritual but not religious" people long for connection with God, they may not want to be bothered with the difficulties of ferreting out the truth of doctrines or theology or the teachings of Scripture. Many are also often disillusioned with the Church and don't want to associate themselves with an institution that has such a troubled history and that includes such flawed people. They want the inspirational moments of spiritual experience without the obligations that come with being a committed member of any organized religion.

Like any other counterfeit god, the god of "spiritual experience" is alluring but is ultimately empty. What good is a "spiritual" experience that is not connected to anything beyond itself? It mimics true relationship with God, and it may temporarily satisfy someone as being almost the same thing, but once it is over the person is no better off than before. The true gospel of Jesus Christ transforms a person, not only temporarily but eternally.

Vague "spiritual experiences" may point toward God and may foreshadow a true relationship with Him, but the difficulties of the Christian life—the suffering, the questioning, the studying of the Bible, the working out of relationships with sometimes troublesome fellow believers, the work of serving others—are just as transformative as the highs of an inspiring spiritual encounter. Being a spiritual person doesn't mean evading the difficulties of religious life—it means engaging them and learning from them.

Not all "spiritual experiences" are related to the reality of God's presence. There are drugs, for instance, that can mimic the kinds of euphoric feelings we associate with powerful encounters with God's presence. Writing about such drug-induced mystical experiences, Christian author Mark Galli asks, "It's a lot of work to fast and pray and worship and deny oneself—and even then, experiencing God is a hit or miss proposition! What's the fuss if we can pop a mushroom and have a nearly guaranteed religious experience?" The fuss, as Galli acknowledges, is that such experiences are meaningless if they are not tied to the truth of the gospel. The focus of Christianity is not euphoric experiences, even though God's presence does sometimes manifest itself that way. Galli writes, "The Christian faith, at its core, is not about ethics or religious experience, but a message about a God who has gone to extraordinary lengths to be and remain on our side, to become the-God-with-a-name, Emmanuel, 'God with us.'"[10]

Go to beaconhillbooks.com for a free downloadable study guide that includes questions for deeper personal reflection as well as activities for use in a small-group setting.

ten ☒ ☒ ☒
GOD IN THE EXTRAORDINARY
The Invisible God at Work

■ One of the Spirit-quenching tendencies of Christians in our age is to try to tame our faith in order to make it look more acceptable and less eccentric to skeptical outsiders. I must admit that I am more comfortable talking about God's presence in the everyday aspects of life, such as music or nature, than in the more unusual and even miraculous manifestations that I want to celebrate throughout the rest of this book.

Like many others, I am so influenced by the naturalistic worldview that is dominant in our culture—the idea that only those things that are observable and provable by *natural* means are true—that I hold what is *super*natural at a distance. I am automatically skeptical of it. If you ascribe something to an encounter with an angel or tell me that someone saw Jesus at the point of death or say that only God's intervention in a situation could have made it come out the way it did, I am likely to be dubious. Is God really the only explanation? Could it have been a coincidence, a faulty perception, wishful thinking? I believe in miracles, but I am suspicious of them when they come.

I think some skepticism is warranted. People do get these things wrong. Some people make up miraculous stories, and others misinterpret what has happened to them. I approach these issues with trepidation. Still, if we are to take our Christian faith seriously, we cannot get away from the supernatural. Even what we consider the most ordinary aspects of our faith are suffused with mind-blowingly audacious claims. What Christian does not believe in prayer? It is a standard element of Christianity, hardly controversial. But what could be more miraculous than prayer? We speak to the Creator of the universe, who actually hears us and responds. What about our belief in the Bible, a book written by humans that contains angels and miracles and prophecies and visions and laws? We believe these things to be true and the book itself to be inspired by God. How radical is that? What about our belief in heaven? Does any Christian deny it, this concept of living millions upon millions of years in a paradise in the very presence of God? It is a staggering belief.

I know Christians who accept these elements of the faith without question and yet would doubt that God ever allowed an angel to intervene in any specific situation in the lives of one of their neighbors. That sounds too outlandish. But the incarnation of God in the form of Jesus Christ? The Transfiguration? The Resurrection? Pentecost? Salvation? These amazing facts have been so toned down and taken for granted that they seem tame and uncontroversial by comparison.

The examples of how God reveals His power in the upcoming pages differ from those earlier in the book not so much because they are more supernatural—*any* revelation of God's presence is supernatural—but rather that they go beyond the experiences of the day-to-day Christian life. Every Christian can enter God's presence by reading Scripture, but only a few may ever encounter an angel. Every Christian can sense God's Spirit in music or in nature, but only a few may be participants in a sweeping revival that transforms a community. These unusual manifestations of God's presence are not at the core of what it means to be a Christian. They are not necessary for salvation. But they do show that God sometimes breaks through the boundaries in breathtaking ways.

God May Be Most Active Even When He's Most Invisible

God is at work all around us in ways we may never know. Scripture is full of stories in which people do not see God or the evidence of His work even when His presence is all around them.

I love the story in 2 Kings in which the king of Aram sends his forces to capture the prophet Elisha. Elisha's servant wakes up in the morning and looks around to see the whole city surrounded with the horses and chariots of the powerful army. Obviously alarmed, the servant asks Elisha, "Oh, my lord, what shall we do?" Elisha isn't a bit worried. He answers, "Don't be afraid. Those who are with us are more than those who are with them." The servant doesn't see it, and neither does Aram's army. Elisha prays, "O Lord, open his eyes so he may see." The Lord does open the servant's eyes, and he sees the *hills full of horses and chariots of fire all around Elisha.*

This makes me wonder, *What forces of God may be all around me right now that I don't see?* I don't think this story indicates that there is *always* an army of horses and chariots of fire around me. But I do believe it shows that some of God's work in my life is invisible. If God showed up in a miraculous way in my life today, would I recognize Him? Would I accept it as a miracle from Him, or would I try to explain it away?

People are not always ready for God's presence when He breaks in to their daily routine:

- Was Moses ready for God to appear to him in the burning bush and give him instructions for leading the Israelites to freedom? He resisted with excuses and insecurity based on what he could see around him rather than on God's supernatural power. Finally he gave in and trusted God's power to guide him.
- Were Zechariah and Elizabeth prepared to become the parents of John the Baptist? When the angel came to Zechariah to announce that Elizabeth would bear a son who would be named John, Zechariah was scared at first, and then he was skeptical. He and his wife were too old. They had received scorn over the years for their barrenness, but wasn't it too late to fix that now? Even though he was working in the Temple itself, where God's supernatural ways are extolled, Zechariah had a hard time accepting the idea that God would break into his own life. The angel struck him speechless throughout the pregnancy as a result of his doubt, but when the baby was born, Zechariah let loose with one of the most beautiful songs recorded in Scripture.
- Was Mary prepared to give birth to the Son of God?
- Was Paul prepared to get knocked off his horse and hear the voice of Jesus on the road to Damascus?

Each of these people, and many others I could mention, had to be awakened to the spiritual realm from which God would intervene to shake up their lives.

What if our lives are not as "ordinary" as we think? As we live out our daily routines, what larger spiritual battles might we be fighting that have consequences far beyond what we will ever witness or imagine? What purposes might God be working out that will be witnessed in realms that are invisible to us?

The Book of Job tells such a story. Job is living out a righteous and prosperous life when the Lord and Satan have a conversation about him. Satan claims that Job loves God only because his circumstances are good and that if God took all that away, Job would curse God to His face.

God allows Satan to take everything from Job—wealth, health, children. Job suffers horribly. He sits and scrapes the sores that cover his body from head to foot and wonders where God is. He wishes he had never been born. No one bothers to tell him about the drama in which he is the main character. He is convinced that God has abandoned him.

In fact, God—and Satan—are watching Job very closely to see what he will do. He feels alone, but he has the most important audience in the world. God is silent, but He is very much *present*. Philip Yancey writes of Job, "Far from being abandoned by God, Job was getting direct, almost microscopic scrutiny from Him. At the very moment Job was pleading for a courtroom trial to present his case, he was actually participating in a trial of cosmic significance—not as the prosecuting attorney jabbing his finger at God, but as the main witness in a test of faith."[1]

God was watching. God was present. God was working, but to Job it seemed exactly the opposite. You don't have to suffer to the extent Job did to know this feeling that God has abandoned you. Who among us has not at some time felt our foundation ripped out from under us? Who has not cried out, *Where are you, God? Why have you done this to me? Why didn't you prevent this? Why have you slammed the door in my face?*

Like Job, in those times we have people around us pushing explanations that don't really explain. Is it possible that in those times when it feels as if God has disappeared, He may in fact be hovering over us intently, watching to see what we'll do, waiting for His own unfathomable timing to intervene? That does not diminish our pain, but it does change its meaning. Is it possible that much of the truth is invisible to us?

The Miracle of "The God Thing"

"That was a God thing" is a statement I occasionally hear from Christian friends. What they mean by it is that circumstances came together in such an unusual and propitious way that only God could have arranged it. It's hard to prove a God thing. God things can be explained away as luck or coincidence or convenient interpretation of a circumstance after the fact. But the large number of these situations and the peculiar details of them convince many Christians that God's fingerprints are all over these patterns of events. They enter your Christian life as a subtle sign or message from God that He is present in your life, no matter how chaotic or difficult it may seem at the moment, and that His guiding hand will lead you through.

One of my most memorable "God thing" moments happened at a Christian writers' conference, where I believe God showed me that He was present but also wanted to teach me a lesson. Several years ago a highly respected editor I knew switched careers to become an agent and was taking on new clients. I really wanted him to represent me, but so did many other writers. I saw this new agent every year at the Mount Hermon Christian Writers Conference, so I hoped for a time to talk to him to see if he would sign me.

The problem at the conference was that the appointment slots for the most popular editors and agents filled up quickly. I had frequently been turned away by someone I wanted to see simply because other writers had already taken all their appointment times. Some schedules were booked within a few hours of the start of the conference. I was determined not to let that happen this time.

My strategy was to snag an appointment with this agent before the conference began. The starting time was at lunch on Friday, but I knew that editors and agents had to check in at a particular desk earlier that morning. I staked it out. I sat on a bench just outside the building where I knew the agent would have to arrive sometime between breakfast and lunch. I didn't care if I had to sit there all morning. I had no intention of leaving my spot until my name was on his appointment schedule.

I tried to be subtle as I stalked him. The Mount Hermon conference center is in a beautiful setting in the midst of towering redwood trees, so it was plausible for me to pretend to be sitting on my bench and enjoying the view. It was a little chilly that morning, and the bench got a little hard after about an hour, but I didn't care. I was going to make this happen. I greeted a few people I knew who came and went, but otherwise I sat and watched. Eventually, I also prayed. *Send this agent, Lord! Make him walk by.*

During normal years at this conference, I would have spent this first morning hiking the trails just beyond the conference center. The trails wind through the majestic trees along the edge of a deep ravine that drops to a stream. There are footbridges and great views all along the trails. I longed to be out there, and the man I was waiting for wasn't showing up. As I prayed, I got no sense that the Lord was going to answer my prayer. My only impression was a feeling of guilt for trying to force this meeting and for wasting a whole morning that could have been spent enjoying the beauty that was a big motivation for traveling here each year.

Instead of answering my prayer in the way I wanted, the only answer I sensed from the Lord was *Stop all this forcing and striving. Trust the Lord to direct your meetings and your future as He has always done. Get off this cold bench and go enjoy the trees.*

Getting off that bench and walking into the forest required all the faith I could muster. I knew it was the right thing to do. My whole little plan felt desperate and petty by this point. But I still pictured my agent walking by this bench the minute I left it.

Still, I did it. I walked away. I prayed, *Lord, for the rest of this conference I'm going to try to relax and trust you with whatever appointments I may or may not get.* I enjoyed the invigorating hike. I gazed high into the massive redwood trees. I smelled the plants and leaves and felt myself relax. I walked down the ravine and listened to the stream. Once lunchtime came, I headed back toward the conference center.

First I decided to stop by my cabin, which was on the way. As I emerged from the woods onto the road where my little house stood, I saw from a distance that someone was leaning on my car. He was talking to someone standing nearby, but I couldn't tell who either person was. Once I got close enough, I saw to my disbelief that the man leaning on my car was the very agent I had spent the whole morning stalking! He reclined there—*on my car, directly in front of my cabin*—talking to one of the top book editors in the publishing industry. I could think of no reason that he should be there. Editors and agents had rooms much closer to the conference center. He and the editor must have been purposely staying away from the commotion of the registration area.

He greeted me as I walked up and introduced me to the editor. He asked me what I was working on these days. In as casual a tone as I could muster, I told him I was actually hoping to get a chance to talk to him about that. I told him I was staying in that cabin just a few feet away and that I had a proposal I would like to give him if I could. He agreed, and I ran to get it. We set an appointment for later in the weekend. As I thanked him and walked away, he and the editor were glancing over my proposal together. Later that weekend he signed me as a client, and he has been my agent ever since.

It's possible to call this a coincidence, but I believe it was a "God thing," a divine appointment. Of all the cars in all the places across that mountain, why was he leaning against *mine*? Why at that moment? Why when I had finally stopped trying to force everything to happen and trust God with my future?

When God Weaves His Presence Through the Tapestry of a Life

God things happen at the level of the individual incident and also at the larger level of the overall span of life. At the larger level, some episodes of life that make no sense when they're happening turn out to have much greater significance when you look back on them years later. Periods of life that feel as if they're dead ends at the moment turn out later to have been important pieces of God's plan for your life.

The broad sweep of my friend Liz's life has more "God thing" interruptions than anyone I know. I remember the buzz of excitement that rippled through our university when

Liz was hired. She had worked for the Library of Congress, had been a researcher for a prominent Christian author, and had been awarded the largest grant the university had ever seen. She had an impressive résumé, but none of it was what she had originally set out to do. God's repeated intervention in her own plans had pushed her in those directions.

Even being a Christian was not part of her original plan. She went to a Christian college not because it was Christian but because it had a good sports program, offered the major she wanted, and was in a good location. She pledged the Christian sorority on campus not because it was Christian but because the girls in it were friendly. She got a job at the campus ministry office not because she was interested in ministry but because she was a graphics artist, and that office was the only place big enough to house her graphics equipment. When someone from the university church offered to pay her way to a missions conference, she accepted only because it was free and she would get a week off school and was told she would not have to make up the homework.

God had higher aspirations for Liz than a week free of homework. She went to the missions conference having never before seen a missionary—she pictured pith helmets and long monastic robes—but questions about Christianity had been bubbling up within her. On the first afternoon of the conference, she met a young man in the student government office who sensed her questioning spirit and asked whether she had any questions about the Bible. She unleashed such a flood of questions that it took most of three days for her new friend not only to answer the questions but to guide her through Scripture so she could see the answers for herself. At the end of those three days he asked whether she was ready to make a decision for Christ. She was ready, and they baptized her at the end of the conference.

After graduation that year she became active in a church with a strong mission focus, particularly in Japan and China. She felt impressed that since God had led her to this church, He must be calling her to one of those countries. She asked her close friends to start praying about which country she should go to—Japan or China—so she could get started in language study.

They did pray. Each of them came to her separately with the results of those prayers and said they thought the Lord was sending her to Washington, D.C.

What? Washington, D.C., was not on the list of options, but that is where God was calling her. Not only her friends' prayers but her own prayers began to confirm this. She thought maybe Washington was somehow to be a kind of training ground for Japan or China, but she didn't know. She agreed to go.

Through another series of God-impelled events she could neither have planned nor foreseen, she landed a university internship in D.C. that had previously been open only to undergraduates. She was their first and only graduate student, and she was assigned to work for a ministry for part of a summer before she was to become a Senate intern. The internship went so well that she was asked to stay on, so she skipped the Senate internship and stayed.

God kept surprising Liz, setting opportunities in her path that were far from her original plans but that had the unmistakable feel of His plan. When the president of the ministry's research assistant left to go to graduate school, Liz took up many of those research duties. Not long after this, she was asked to become the organization's librarian, so her career took a whole new path. She pursued a graduate degree in library science while working at the ministry, which also now included helping prepare research for what became a best-selling book. While in her graduate studies, she began to sense what seemed to her like an odd call—to evangelize librarians. She says, "You kind of know this has to be from God when it's this unusual!" But how do you evangelize librarians?

Shortly after the book came out, Liz received a phone call from the woman who had the top librarian appointment in the federal government. She had just read the new book, including the author's nice comments about Liz in the back, and was interested in hiring Liz for a position that would entail writing speeches to librarians and scholars internationally and, when possible, to include the writings of Christian authors such as C. S. Lewis, G. K. Chesterton, Paul Tournier, and others. Liz wrote speeches and articles for commencements, conferences, and to leaders in the library profession. That position led to another job, this time with the Library of Congress.

Coincidence or "God thing"?

Liz finally felt settled in her personal and professional life and thought she might spend the rest of her life in the Washington, D.C., area. She says, "I was pretty crazy about a special man, my work and ministry, my church, and close friendships." Around this time a friend asked her where she would move if God were going to move her anywhere. Liz says that for reasons she didn't fully understand, she replied very quickly that if God *were* going to move her, it would be to a university that had a seminary, and she would direct the seminary library and teach pastors how to use technology more effectively in their ministries.

Then she and her friend had a good laugh, because she had no experience in that area, knew of no such jobs, and had no desire or intention to move. Two hours later her friend sent her a job posting from Azusa Pacific University in California. They were seeking someone to start a seminary library and be the associate university librarian. The person needed to have strong technology skills to train pastors how to be more effective in their ministry. She could not deny that God was at work again and felt she had to apply for this job. Within three days of sending the application, she received a call for an interview. A few weeks later she came to campus to meet the search committee and was offered the job within the first hour of her visit to the campus. She has been at APU ever since, fulfilling the mission she had blurted out to a friend in faith years earlier.

It's easy to see God's hand at work in Liz's life when you look at the big picture. His guidance at every major step looks unmistakable. Of course, this wide-angle view leaves out many important details. It leaves out the setbacks, the doubts, the crises, the battles, the disappointments, the pain. In the middle of any particular episode of life, God's presence may be harder to sense. I see evidence of God's movement in my past, but the present looks more chaotic and insecure. Part of my faith is to believe, despite all the conflicting signals around me, that He is still guiding me now as He did then. I keep moving forward in the faith that someday I will be able to look back and see what He was up to during this tumultuous period. Even when looking into the past, not all of it makes sense. Perhaps some of it was wasted time, and some of it will make sense only from the even larger perspective of eternity.

God leaves evidence of His presence not only in the big moments of life but also in the small details—a meeting with just the right person at just the right time, a message from someone who may not even know its significance, an overheard song that is exactly what you need to hear, and a thousand other examples.

In Liz's story, for instance, God's sense of humor showed through during her early days in Washington, D.C. With little money to live on, Liz asked for prayer from a group she was associated with to find a place to rent. That prayer was answered when she moved into a tiny apartment with two other young women. The girls had little more than a mattress, a wooden crate, and a pan to cook with. Liz asked for more prayer and posted a note at the ministry offices that she needed help with furniture, and by that afternoon the apartment was fully furnished with living room furniture, a dining room table and chairs, a bed, a dresser, dishes, and silverware. People arrived in a steady stream all day to donate items. Her new roommates were astonished at the power of prayer! One of them joked that now all she needed to do was get busy and pray for a lamp for the living room and an ironing board.

A week later Liz attended a prayer meeting at a new church and told how God had worked out so many details in her move to Washington. Afterward a woman came up to her and insisted on giving her a few more items for her apartment. What were they?

Two living room lamps and an ironing board!

God things are unpredictable. Christians may go years without any discernible signs like these. They may not happen at all for some people, or if they do happen, people may fail to recognize them. I believe God spreads some of these throughout our lives as signs of love and connection, the way a friend might leave a card or a small gift as a token of encouragement. In a time of confusion or discouragement, a God thing might offer just enough hope to keep you going. It might reassure you that, in spite of the battle, God is still there, still ultimately in control.

Go to beaconhillbooks.com for a free downloadable study guide that includes questions for deeper personal reflection as well as activities for use in a small-group setting.

eleven ⊠ ⊠ ⊠
GOD IN THE EXTRAORDINARY
Shaken by Revival, Touched by Angels, Approaching the Eternal

■ Imagine this: an 8.0 earthquake rocks southern California, causing widespread panic and destruction throughout Los Angeles and surrounding areas. Hundreds of people die, buildings fall, freeways buckle, millions lose water and electricity. Thousands are homeless. In the aftermath, as communities begin to rebuild and people strive to put their lives back together, something unexpected happens.

Across the region, people fill quake-damaged churches on Sunday mornings in numbers never seen before. The disaster has forced thousands of people out of their spiritual complacency and has brought spiritual questions of life, death, and eternity into sharper focus. Young people in their twenties are at the forefront of this movement to sweep aside the trivialities of life and confront what is most important. Pastors of every denomination are caught off guard not only by the numbers of newcomers to their churches but also by the spiritual hunger of the seekers. As the weeks go by, hundreds of people, and then thousands, are converted to belief in Christ.

Word of this spiritual awakening spreads across the United States, and similar spikes in church attendance and conversions to Christianity happen in Dallas, Chicago, Boston, and other cities. Within a few months, starting mostly on university campuses and moving outward from there, cities in England and France also report greater church attendance. Some congregations that had been all but spiritually dead now spring to life again.

Revival has broken out in the world.

Many people alive today have never witnessed such a dramatic movement of the Holy Spirit as I have just described. What would happen if the Holy Spirit swept through an entire nation or region of the world? Such revivals have happened around the world throughout the centuries, even during our lifetime. Revivals may also happen in more limited forms within particular churches or college campuses. Revivals are unpredictable. The conditions that create them during one era may not do so in another. But sometimes these powerful movements of the Holy Spirit are ushered in by the prayers of the Church and the determination of people to seek Him out and not to settle for the more usual casual approach to faith. How many are praying for revival today?

When God Shakes Up the World

The revival scenario I painted is patterned on another famous revival that happened almost three hundred years ago. Some say the Great Awakening that swept the United States and England began with a rare earthquake on October 29, 1727, in New England. The quake was not terribly destructive but did bring down parts of buildings and shook many of the residents out of their complacency. In that deeply religious age, the people understood that earthquakes had natural causes but also believed God sometimes used such events to send a message. They began to seek out what that message might be.

Although the seeds of revival may have been planted then, the revival itself did not burst forth until a few years later. Like the hypothetical revival story I created, the revival that began in Northampton, Massachusetts, started among the young people. Jonathan Edwards, one of the greatest religious figures of his time, was pastor of the Congregational church and wrote about the revival in a work that would itself spark other revivals elsewhere in the world, *A Faithful Narrative of the Surprising Work of God*.

For a long time Edwards had been concerned about the downward moral slide of the young people in his congregation, especially those in their twenties. As Edwards' biographer, George Marsden, explains, men and women were postponing marriage during that era to an average age of twenty-nine for men and twenty-five for women. They did so mostly for economic reasons, due to a shortage of available land that would make it possible for them to earn a living and start a family. The youth culture that developed among these twenty-somethings included Sunday night "frolics" and "company keeping" that sometimes led to sexual promiscuity and other sins.[1] Edwards was also concerned about the disrespect these young people showed in the worship services.

But in late 1733, Edwards began to notice a shift in attitude in these young people. Two unexpected deaths in the community the following year served to continue to shift the young people's minds toward spiritual matters as they contemplated the fragility and brevity of life. They began to meet together in the evenings after services to take part in "social religion," or times of discussion, Bible study, and prayer. The revival that had bubbled up among the youth spread to the older members of the congregation who also started meeting together for similar times of prayer and spiritual renewal.

In December 1734, as Edwards tells it, "the spirit of God began extraordinarily to set in, and wonderfully to work amongst us; and there were, very suddenly, one after another, five or six persons, who were to all appearance savingly converted, and some of them wrought upon in a very remarkable manner."[2] One surprising conversion in particular had an impact on the church's young people. A young woman who had been "one of the greatest company-keepers in the whole town" told of God's transformation of her life. Edwards writes that the news hit "like a flash of lightning" on the hearts of people throughout the town.

Over the next several months, the entire focus of the townspeople shifted to spiritual matters. "There was scarcely a single person in the town, old or young, left unconcerned about the great things of the eternal world," wrote Edwards. "Those who were wont to be the vainest, and loosest; and those who had been most disposed to think, and speak slightly of vital and experimental religion, were now generally subject to great awakenings."[3] Hundreds of conversions followed. The town was filled with the presence of God, plus joy and love. People began to treat others better. Families rejoiced together. Visitors to the town were swept up in God's saving power. The revival spread to other towns throughout the region.

News of the revival spread far beyond Northampton when Edwards wrote his account of the events in his town. He wrote a narrative of the revival in a letter to the influential pastor Benjamin Colman in Boston, who sent it to influential pastors in England, including hymn writer Isaac

Watts. Other versions of Edwards' account were published in America, England, and elsewhere over the next few years. Revival spread. Edwards' narrative did not arrive in a vacuum. God was already working in the ministries of other remarkable Christians, including John and Charles Wesley and evangelist George Whitefield, all of whom were influenced by Edwards' narrative.

Whitefield, after preaching to huge crowds in England, came to America in 1739 and also preached to tens of thousands of people eager to hear the gospel. In the Northampton revival, Edwards had been struck by the spiritual hunger of the people, whose daily conversations had turned from the mundane to the spiritual. The same was true when Whitefield preached, as indicated by the enormous crowds. In Boston, for example, fifteen thousand people turned out to hear his outdoor sermon on Boston Common on September 18, 1740. A little more than a month later, twenty thousand people came to hear him. Those are huge numbers considering that the entire population of Boston was seventeen thousand and also considering that he spoke to them in an era before microphones and speakers that would have made it easier to hear.[4]

Benjamin Franklin befriended Whitefield, and though he wasn't so interested in the preacher's theology, he was impressed by the man's ability to make himself heard by so many people. Franklin used his own scientific methods to calculate that Whitefield could be heard by as many as thirty thousand people at a time. As impressive as that is, from the standpoint of revival it is even more impressive that so many would *want* to hear a sermon. Revival had taken hold, and lives were changed. Even the skeptical Franklin acknowledged that people's lives were changed. He wrote, "It was wonderful to see the change soon made in the manners of our inhabitants. From being thoughtless or indifferent about religion, it seem'd as if all the world were growing religious, so that one could not walk thro' the town in an evening without hearing psalms sung in different families of every street."[5]

As inspiring and transformative as these revivals sound, there were also problems. They faded. The Northampton revival was brought to an abrupt halt when Edwards' own uncle, Joseph Hawley, who suffered from mental illness, slit his own throat, in part because of his despair over lack of assurance of his salvation. After this suicide, other people in the town also faced temptations to cut their own throats. A few did so. Edwards saw these strange reactions as Satan's way of fighting against the powerful work the Holy Spirit was doing. Revival is spiritual battle, and evil forces will be arrayed against it. Edwards still believed that the good that came out of the revival in terms of the true transformation of lives outweighed the tragic incidents that were connected to it.

Another danger of revivals, both in Edwards' day and ours, is that emotionalism can overshadow the authentic work of the Holy Spirit. Some people get so swept up in the intensity of the crowd and the thrill of so many people uniting in worship that the responses can turn sensationalistic and overwrought. Once the emotion fades, some find that they have done little real spiritual work. For them, the impact of the revival vanishes as soon as the emotion does. In spite of that danger, many others may draw closer to Christ in ways that will permanently change their lives and their churches.

True revival cannot be forced. We don't know where or when the Holy Spirit's power will break out in unusually powerful ways. But revival can be prepared for. Many of the most famous revivals have been preceded by years of prayer. Many revivals start small, as the Northampton one did, one with a group of young people "waking up" spirituality and deciding to set aside trivialities in favor of pursuing things that really matter.

Round-the-Clock Revival

Closer to our own day, another revival started with a group of young people turning to God in prayer and expectation. On February 3, 1970, students gathered for chapel at Asbury College in Wilmore, Kentucky. Chapel was a routine event, just as it is at other Christian colleges around the world. This one was scheduled to begin at 10 A.M. and end one hour later. In fact, that chapel service did not end until a week later, and before it was over, revival had spread far beyond that small college across several states. The story of it continues to inspire people today.

The chapel began simply enough. The dean of the college spoke, but instead of giving a sermon, he gave his testimony. He then opened up the service to others to tell what Christ was doing in their lives. As one student after another came up to speak, the Holy Spirit moved into the service with unusual power. An invitation was given for people to pray at the altar, and many did. The testimonies continued, and so did the singing and praying. The time came to end the service, but no one was ready to leave. Another hour went by, and then another, and still people prayed and sang and confessed and told their stories of God's work.[6]

Dennis Kinlaw was president of Asbury College at that time, but on that morning when revival started, he had to fly to Canada for a meeting. When he reached his hotel late in the day, he had an urgent message to call home. He reached the dean of the college at 7 P.M. The dean informed him, "The chapel isn't over yet." Kinlaw asked, "What do you mean the chapel isn't over? It's seven o'clock at night!" In fact, the revival was just beginning. As word spread, the news media found out what was happening and came to cover the story. College officials feared cynicism or mockery from the media, but instead, the reporters were amazed by what they saw.

As the service continued around the clock, hundreds of people came from across Kentucky, Indiana, and Michigan to witness the revival and take part in it. Dr. Kinlaw was gone for the first several days of the revival, but even in Canada the power of revival reached him. At one point he called home from a phone booth, and he says that he had never felt such a strong sense of God's presence as he did in that booth. "I was encompassed in God," he said as he told the story years later.[7] When he flew home, he went directly from the airport to the campus at 2:30 in the morning. The closer he got to Asbury, the stronger he felt God's presence.

The revival was about more than simply *sensing* God's presence. The Holy Spirit changed the lives of students and faculty and visitors. Kinlaw said that in the testimonies he heard, there was an emphasis on sin and the need for repentance and restitution. People confessed to those they had wronged. They healed relationships. They brought their lives into obedience to what they knew God wanted them to do.

Then the revival spread around the country as students went to their hometowns and elsewhere to tell what was happening at Asbury. Many would go to churches and simply ask for a few minutes to tell about the revival. Kinlaw said that in many churches once the students told their stories, the revival would start happening there also. These were not flashy presentations but simple stories told by regular students. Kinlaw said, "It was almost the less impressive the student was, the more effective as an instrument he was." He heard of one shy young woman who spoke one day in five churches, and over two hundred people responded. The college began getting calls from churches with no Asbury connection to have students come to tell their stories. They went to other college campuses and churches of varying denominations.

The round-the-clock chapel service ended after a week, but the effects of the revival in terms of changed lives were felt for years. Why did it happen? Revivals are a mystery. It's impossible to know why the Holy Spirit breaks forth in one time and place and not another. But fervent prayer is one element identified as a precursor to many revivals, and it was happening at Asbury. In the dormitories and elsewhere, students and others had been praying for months for true revival to come. They expected it to come. They were ready to respond when the Holy Spirit shifted them out of their normal routines.

Revival could happen anywhere, and it *is* happening in various places all over the world. Some lament what they see as the decline of Christianity, but maybe they are looking in the wrong places. Mark Shaw in his recent book on global revivals over the last hundred years points out that in 1900 Africa had 10 million Christians. By 2000 the number had exploded to 400 hundred million Christians. He tells the stories of revivals that have occurred over the past hundred years in Korea, Nigeria, India, Brazil, Ghana, China and elsewhere.[8] God honors the humble, persistent prayers of His people. The Holy Spirit has never stopped working.

Will you see revival in your lifetime? In the area where I live, I not only *don't* see revival, but I don't even hear people talking about it or longing for it. I know few people who use the term, and many younger Christians may not even have much idea what it means. That could change, and it won't necessarily take some cataclysm like an earthquake to usher it in. What might happen if small groups of people in churches around the nation gathered together specifically to pray for revival? Who will be willing to step forward in their own churches to call Christians to pray?

Approaching the Eternal Realm

Revelation is a stunning book of the Bible. John's vision looks into realms normally shut off to us during this lifetime. He sees angels. He sees the New Jerusalem coming down out of heaven. He sees the river of the water of life flowing through that city. He sees the tree of life with its twelve crops of fruit growing beside that river. With a mixture of literal and symbolic imagery, he gives us a glimpse into eternity.

A veil usually hides this eternal realm from people, but John is allowed to see through. In a smaller way, I believe the veil is lifted back a bit at times for us as well, as we've seen throughout this book. On a regular basis it may be lifted back as we pray, as we worship God through music, as we love and serve others in His name. At rare times the veil may be lifted back for some people in more unusual ways, such as in an encounter with an angel or a glimpse into eternity at the point of death. We can't *expect* these kinds of incidents, and we need to consider that sometimes there are alternate explanations for some of them, but we can enjoy these gifts when they come.

Angels Watching over Me

Today many people, including Christians, are skeptical that angels play much of a role in our world or that they even exist, but in Scripture they are widely discussed. Angels are mentioned more than three hundred times in the Bible. They serve many functions. They send messages. They give warnings. They guide people through danger. They bring hope. They bring destruction. They worship God. They represent God. They rescue people. They make announcements. They comfort people.

Sometimes angels in Scripture are visible to those around them, but at other times, as in the story of Balaam's donkey or the story of Elisha's servant Gehazi, the angels are invisible, at least until God allows a person's eyes to be opened to them. In the encounters with angels that people describe today, they are sometimes visible to certain people but not to others. In a typical example from Robert Strand's collection of dozens of stories he gathered from people who have encountered angels, a man who owned a sporting goods store in an isolated part of town felt threatened by a gang of young men riding motorcycles outside his store. One of them came inside and asked questions about the guns the man sold, but the owner refused to sell him one. The next day, while the owner was in the store alone, the gang came roaring back, and Robert expected trouble. Instead, the young men simply rode around in circles outside the store for a while and then took off.

Later, one of the owner's regular customers came in and said he came by earlier but left because he saw through the window that the store was full of customers. The owner knew, however, that no one else had been in the store at that time of day. He believes the "customers" the man saw—and that kept the gang away—were angels.[9]

It's surprising how many angel encounters have to do with travel and crises that happen on the road, as if helping travelers is a particular role of angels. Strand devotes a whole section of his book to angel stories of this type. Even in the Bible, angels are often connected to journeys. When the Israelites made their way to the Promised Land, God told them, "See, I am sending an angel ahead of you to guard you along the way and to bring you to the place I have prepared. Pay attention to him and listen to what he says" (Exodus 23:20-21).

My wife encountered a man she believes was an angel on a challenging journey up a mountain near our home. She and a friend of ours planned to take our kids up the mountain to a weekend winter camp. Several cars from our church were going up, and normally the drive to the camp was a pleasant and easy journey.

On this Friday night, however, rain was the first sign of trouble. The rain would be snow higher up the mountain, so everyone was required to pull over at a certain spot to put chains on the tires. Someone helped my wife and her friend with this after they waited in a long line, but the wait took its toll on the battery of our friend's SUV, and the battery died before they were able to go any farther up the mountain. They had to wait for a battery jump, and by then the snow was falling hard.

The car continued to crawl up the mountain, but before they made it up to the camp, the police closed the road and sent everyone back down. Our daughter was already farther up the mountain in another car, but cell phone service was spotty, and my wife couldn't reach her. Back down the mountain my wife and her friend came, and they had to get the chains off the tires before they could drive on the streets below. When they pulled into the area where they had put on the chains going up, no one was there. It was dark. It was snowing. They feared the battery might die again. The phones weren't working. They were stuck.

That's when the angel came.

My wife believes he was an angel because he came from "out of nowhere" and lay down in the rain on the side of the road and began to take the chains off. Taking off chains requires a process of moving the car forward and backward, and my wife stood outside the car and directed her friend in this process as the "angel" lay on the ground and removed the chains. The man was drenched. He didn't say much but stayed focused on the task at hand. Once the chains were off, my wife turned to thank him, but he was gone. She hadn't seen where he came from, didn't know why he had stopped to help, and didn't know where he went once he finished.

Many angel stories involve "people" who could not have been where they were. Strand tells the story of a couple who desperately needed to get their sick son to a hospital. Snowdrifts blocked most of the roads in their area of Colorado, and the hospital was thirty miles away. They prepared their truck as best they could and headed out. Snow plows had been out, so they were able to travel for a while, but then they saw something ominous—a broken-down snowplow stranded by the side of the highway. If even a snowplow couldn't make it, how would they? They reluctantly continued over unplowed roads, but it wasn't long before part of their truck slid into a hole caused by a collapsed portion of the highway.

Now they were *really* stuck, and their son was getting sicker. They prayed for rescue. It came in an unexpected form. Looking behind them, they heard the snowplow—the same one they had seen abandoned by the side of the road—barreling toward them. The young man who drove it stopped and offered to help them. First he got out a chain and pulled their truck out of the hole, and then he offered to drive in front of them and plow a path to the hospital. That's what he did, and their son got the treatment he needed.

Wanting to thank the man who had helped them, the couple called the county maintenance office and asked for the driver's name so they could do something for him. The man's supervisor was confused. The transmission of the snowplow they were referring to had broken down the day before, and the driver had been sent home. The plow was still stranded, and the driver was waiting on a new one. If someone had rescued them, it hadn't been anyone who worked for the county.[10]

Encounters with angels—at least those that people are aware of—are rare. Before I started asking people about them, I would have thought they were even more unusual than they are. As people I know have learned that I was planning to write about this, some have told their own stories of incidents they suspect included the work of angels. My friend Harvey isn't sure who prompted him to make a life-saving decision as a teenager. Was it an angel? The Holy Spirit? Or simply a coincidence in which he showed good sense? Harvey was riding with his brother Mark down an isolated country road in a farm area near Emporia, Kansas. His brother was driving and had his seatbelt on, but Harvey didn't. Wearing a seatbelt wasn't as standard in that era of the 1960s, and Harvey was a teenager who felt indestructible. Besides, on a country road with few other cars, why would he need to be strapped in?

That day, however, for reasons he still doesn't understand, he sensed an inner voice telling him to put on that seatbelt. He did so, and the reason soon became apparent. His brother came upon a slow-moving car driven by an elderly woman. His brother pulled to her left to pass her, but as soon as his car was parallel with hers, she suddenly turned left onto a dirt road. Harvey's brother swerved left to avoid her, and his car plunged into a ditch. The car rolled over and left the two boys hanging upside down—by their seatbelts. "If I hadn't been wearing my seatbelt," said Harvey, "I would have been ejected from the car and it would have been all over." As it turned out, the boys were not badly injured. Harvey sees it as a miracle of God's protection, one of many in his life.

Stories like this may happen once or twice in a lifetime, if at all. Sometimes people are unsure about them and reluctant even to tell about them, because the angel they're telling about *could* have been a person. I ran across a story, for instance, of a man who brought food to a needy family, but when the family went to try to find him to thank him, he was gone. There are various stories of unseen angels lifting someone up after an accident or pushing someone out of harm's way at the last moment. Do these stories really describe people or angels? Doesn't God use both as He answers prayers and gives provision to His people? Much of the work of angels is behind the scenes, hidden from our awareness most of the time, as Scripture shows. We can't *expect* to encounter them, but it's a thrill when it happens, an encouraging glimpse beyond the veil.

A Peek into Eternity

Trudy Harris is a hospice care nurse who for more than thirty years has cared for patients as they passed from life to death. Her descriptions of the days and hours leading up to the death of her patients show that for many, the veil between the present and eternity is particularly thin just before a person crosses over. As she writes in her book *Glimpses of Heaven*, "I have the feeling that people do not die at the exact minute or hour that we say they do. In some

inexplicable way that we do not yet understand, they seem
to travel back and forth from this world to the next, develop-
ing the insights God wants them to have on this, their final
journey back to the Father who created them."[11]

It is not uncommon for people at the point of death to
see angels in their rooms. It's also common for them to have
visions of loved ones who have died and to hear beautiful
music and smell fragrant flowers. Harris, who has sat with
many patients experiencing these visions, at first assumed
they must be the result of medications or dehydration. But
then she noticed that the same things happened with patients who were not on medication and not dehydrated.
That's when she "started to listen, really listen." The angels
people describe have a similar look—tall and wearing "lu-
minescent" white unlike anything the people have seen.

When one patient asked Harris whether the angel was
really in the room, Harris answered bluntly, "Yes . . . when
you see that angel, he is really here in the room with you. . .
. God often lets people have glimpses of heavenly beings before they get there." Harris's many experiences with people
seeing through the veil into eternity have convinced her that
many of them have been given a heightened spiritual perception, what she calls "spiritual eyes and ears," and they are
allowed to see things hidden from the rest of us most of the
time. She writes, "We can try to explain these things away in
lofty, scientific terms, but eventually we come to know that
we are not meant to understand everything. In time that is
a relief, since we no longer waste time trying to give our understanding and meaning to a dying person's experiences."[12]

In books such as *Heaven Is for Real* and *90 Minutes in
Heaven*, a few people have told of near-death experiences in
which they cross into heaven for a short time before being
brought back to life. Their vivid descriptions of what they

saw and experienced have been enormously popular, with those two books in particular hitting the tops of bestseller lists for many weeks. They have also triggered skepticism among both Christian and non-Christian readers. Christian critics of the books have wondered if God really allows such temporary forays into heaven. Do these experiences conform to what Scripture teaches about the afterlife? Can there be alternate explanations for such experiences?

I have been skeptical of some of these accounts, but one that I found compelling was Don Piper's *90 Minutes in Heaven*. Paramedics declared Piper dead at the scene of a terrible car accident. They covered him with a tarp. He lay there for ninety minutes as a preacher who had come upon the scene prayed over his body. He was revived, and the book is his story of what happened during those ninety minutes and his slow and difficult recovery that followed. Piper went to heaven during those minutes, or at least the outskirts of it, and I found his description of what he experienced inspiring. I read it shortly after reading Randy Alcorn's *Heaven*, which analyzes what the Bible teaches about the afterlife. What Piper heard and saw brought to life the concepts Alcorn had explored in Scripture.

Piper finds it frustrating to try to describe heaven because words can't do justice to its perfection. He writes that everything he experienced was like "a first-class buffet for the senses." Time had no meaning there, even though he now has to describe his experience in terms of time. He was welcomed by his grandfather, by a childhood friend who had died at age nineteen, and many others. Two of the most striking things about heaven were the light and the music. The light was brilliant, intense and inviting beyond earthly description. It got brighter as he moved toward the gate of heaven itself (which he never went through). "Strange as it seems," he writes, "as brilliant as everything was, each time I stepped forward, the splendor increased. The farther I walked, the brighter the light. The light engulfed me, and I had the sense I was being ushered into the presence of God."[13]

The music of heaven had the greatest impact on Piper. He said, "It was the most beautiful and pleasant sound I've ever heard, and it didn't stop. . . . I didn't just hear music. It seemed as if I were part of the music—and it played in and through my body. I stood still, and yet I felt embraced by the sounds." In ways that are hard to explain in earthly terms, he could hear hundreds of songs all at the same time, yet they all blended together perfectly in ways that would be impossible here. In that blend of music were songs he knew and songs he had never heard before. The music filled him with the greatest joy he had ever known.[14]

What interests me almost as much as the experiences is thinking about why they are so popular. Why have so many millions of readers been drawn to these books? I believe a longing for heaven is built into us, and these accounts touch that homesickness for our true home. Even though we spend so much of life in denial of life's brevity, some part of us feels a tug toward the place where we will soon go for eternity. Even though Piper spent only minutes in that place, he immediately felt at home there. He wants to go back. He wants to hear the music again. "I was home," he writes. "I was where I belonged. I wanted to be there more than I had ever wanted to be anywhere on earth. . . . I had no needs, and I felt perfect."[15]

With all these unusual ways that people may see through the veil—encounters with angels, glimpses of heaven, and others—it's important never to let them replace the core message of the gospel. Maybe that's the very reason they're rare, so that we don't begin to worship the miraculous experience rather than Jesus Christ himself. The Bible keeps bringing us back to the core message of salvation in Christ. These other manifestations of God's presence are inspiring, but not necessary for living the Christian life. Even the most amazing encounter with an angel will not save us. Only Jesus can do that. Edith M. Humphrey writes,

> In the light of what God has done in Christ, there is no need for us to go far afield to find ultimate reality. We need neither to ascend to the realms of heaven nor trek down to the abyss (Romans 10:5-7), nor need we search feverishly for methods, spiritual techniques, and unseen power. For this One who is the very active Word of God is near us: indeed he has visited us, has plunged into the matter of this world, rescued us from the darkest regions, and now dwells intimately with us through the Spirit. It is due to *his* questing, *his* agony, and *his* victory that "everyone who calls upon the name of the Lord shall be saved" (Romans 10:13).[16]

God is all around us. He is waiting. If you want to find Him, pick up a Bible and start reading. Turn to Him in prayer. Find a church filled with people who follow Jesus Christ, and join their fellowship. Sing a song of praise to God. He will find you. Before you ever sought Him, He was already moving toward you.

Go to beaconhillbooks.com for a free downloadable study guide that includes questions for deeper personal reflection as well as activities for use in a small-group setting.

NOTES

Chapter 1

1. *Raiders of the Lost Ark*, motion picture, directed by Steven Spielberg (Los Angeles: Paramount, 1981).

Chapter 2

1. Timothy Stafford, *Surprised by Jesus: His Agenda for Changing Everything in A.D. 30 and Today* (Downers Grove, Ill.: Intervarsity Press, 2006), 125-26.

2. Marilynne Robinson, *Absence of Mind* (New Haven, Conn.: Yale University Press, 2010), xxxvii.

3. Francis S. Collins, *The Language of God: A Scientist Presents Evidence for Belief* (New York: Free Press, 2006), 6.

4. Ibid., 6.

5. Dallas Willard, *Knowing Christ Today: Why We Can Trust Spiritual Knowledge* (New York: Harper One, 2009), 144.

6. Monica Ganas, *Under the Influence: California's Intoxicating Spiritual and Cultural Impact on America* (Grand Rapids: Brazos Press, 2010), 99.

7. Ibid., 92-93.

8. Rob Moll, "A Culture of Resurrection," *Christianity Today*, June 7, 2010. <http:/www.christianitytoday.com/ct/article_print.html?id =87979>.

9. Randy Alcorn, *Heaven* (Wheaton, Ill.: Tyndale House Publishers, 2004), 10.

10. Ibid., 171-72.

Chapter 3

1. Frank C. Laubach, *Letters by a Modern Mystic* (Westwood, N.J.: Fleming H. Revell, 1937), 20.

2. Ibid., 10.

3. Ibid., 16, 29.

4. Ibid., 16.

5. Willard, *Knowing Christ Today*, 142.

6. Dalton Conley, "Wired for Distraction?" *Time*, February 21, 2011, 55-56.

7. Suzanne Choney, "Average American Teen Sends and Receives 3,339 Texts a Month," MSNBC.com, October 14, 2010, <http://technology.msnbc.msn.com/_news/2010/10/14/5290191-average-american-teen-sends-and-receives-3339-texts-a-month>.

Chapter 4

1. Clare Booth Luce, quoted in Hugh T. Kerr and John M. Mulder, ed., *Famous Conversions* (Grand Rapids: Wm. B. Eerdmans, 1999), 249.

2. Karl W. Giberson, *Saving Darwin: How to Be a Christian and Believe in Evolution* (New York: HarperCollins, 2008), 209.

3. Ibid., 210.

4. Curt Suplee, "The Sun: Living with a Stormy Star," *National Geographic*, July 2004, 17.

5. MoniBasu, "Scientists Discover Monster Star," CNN.com, July 10, 2010. <http://www.cnn.com/2010/WORLD/europe/07/21/monster.star/index.html?iref=allsearch>.

6. Andrew Fazekas, "Black Hole Hosts Universe's Most Massive Water Cloud," July 28, 2011, *National Geographic Daily News.* <http://news.nationalgeographic.com/news/2011/07/110726-most-massive-water-cloud-quasar-black-hole-space-science/>.

7. "Galaxies," *National Geographic Science.* <http://science.nationalgeographic.com/science/space/universe/galaxies-article/?source=A-to-Z>.

Chapter 5

1. Marius von Senden, quoted in Annie Dillard, *Pilgrim at Tinker Creek* (New York: Book-of-the-Month Club, 1990), 25-26.

2. Ibid., 27.

3. Ibid., 28-29.

4. Richard Stearns, *The Hole in Our Gospel* (Nashville: Thomas Nelson, 2010), 135.

5. Mother Teresa, quoted in "Mother Teresa," *Catholic Planet*, July 21, 2011.

<http://www.catholicplanet.com/articles/article115.htm>.

6. Barbara Brown Taylor, *An Altar in the World: A Geography of Faith* (New York: HarperOne, 2009), 27.

7. Ibid., 102.

8. Stafford, *Surprised by Jesus*, 196.

Chapter 6

1. Joseph Bentz, *Song of Fire* (Nashville: Thomas Nelson, 1995), 7.

2. John Koessler, "The Trajectory of Worship," *Christianity Today*, March 2011, 20-21.

3. Mark Moring, "Pop Goes the Worship," interview with T. David Gordon, *Christianity Today*, March 2011, 22-25.

4. Lawrence R. Mumford, "A Variety of Religious Composition," *Christianity Today*, June 22, 2011. <http://www.christianitytoday.com/ct/2011/june/varietyreligious.html>.

5. Joel Hartse, "Groans Too Deep for Words," *Christianity Today*, January 2009, 54-55.

Chapter 7

1. Jodi Werhanowicz, *Rogue Angel* (Phoenix: Ezekiel Press, 2005), 65, 87-88, 128.

2. Charles G. Finney, *Memoirs of Rev. Charles G. Finney* (New York: A. S. Barnes & Company, 1876), 16-17.

3. Barbara Reynolds, *Dorothy L. Sayers: Her Life and Soul* (London: Hodder & Stoughton, 1993), 368.

4. Dennis P. Hollinger, *Head, Heart & Hands: Bringing Together Christian Thought, Passion and Action* (Downers Grove, Ill.: Intervarsity Press, 2005), 58.

5. Taylor, *An Altar in the World*, 43.

6. Dean Nelson, *God Hides in Plain Sight: How to See the Sacred in a Chaotic World* (Grand Rapids: Brazos Press, 2009), 68.

7. Thornton Wilder, *Three Plays: Our Town, The Skin of Our Teeth, The Matchmaker* (New York: Harper & Brothers, 1957), 100.

Chapter 8

1. Stafford, *Surprised by Jesus*, 60.

2. Robert Alter, *The First Five Books of Moses: A Translation with Commentary* (New York: Norton, 2004), 505.

3. Ibid., 460.

4. Ibid., 476.

5. Frank A. James III, "In the Shadow of Mount Hood," *Christianity Today*, October 5, 2010. <http://www.christianitytoday.com/ct/article_print.html?id=89635>.

Chapter 9

1. Tom Bissell, *Extra Lives: Why Video Games Matter* (New York: Pantheon Books, 2010), 4.

2. Ibid., 159-60.

3. Ibid., 166.

4. Ibid., 182.

5. Gerald G. May, M.D., *Addiction and Grace: Love and Spirituality in the Healing of Addictions* (New York: HarperCollins, 1988), 1.

6. Ganas, *Under the Influence,* 76.

7. Ibid., 79.

8. John Blake, "Are There Dangers in Being 'Spiritual but Not Religious'?" CNN.com, June 5, 2010. <http://cnn.site.printthis.clickability.com/pt/cpt?action=cpt&title=Are+t...%2Fspiritual.but.not.religious%2Findex.html%3Fhpt%3DC1&partnerID=211911>.

9. Taylor, *An Altar in the World,* xiii.

10. Mark Galli, "The End of Christianity as We Know It," *Christianity Today,* April 15, 2010. <http://www.christianitytoday.com/ct/article_print.html?ide=87431>.

Chapter 10

1. Philip Yancey, *Disappointment with God* (Grand Rapids: Zondervan Publishing House, 1988), 264.

Chapter 11

1. George Marsden, *A Short Life of Jonathan Edwards* (Grand Rapids: Wm. B. Eerdmans Publishing Co., 2008), Kindle edition, chapter 4, "The Awakening."

2. Jonathan Edwards, "A Faithful Narrative of the Surprising Work of God," in *Basic Writings,* ed. Ola Elizabeth Winslow (New York: Signet Classic, 1966), 99.

3. Ibid., 101.

4. Collin Hansen and John Woodbridge, *A God-Sized Vision: Revival Stories That Stretch and Stir* (Grand Rapids: Zondervan Publishing House, 2010), Kindle edition, chapter 2, "'Surprising' Signs of the New Birth: First Great Awakening, 1730s to 1740s."

5. Benjamin Franklin, quoted in Walter Isaacson, ed., *A Benjamin Franklin Reader* (New York: Simon and Schuster, 2003), 489.

6. "A Revival Account: Asbury 1970," YouTube Video. <http://www.youtube.com/watch?v=7qOqitIKUNs>.

7. Ibid.

8. Mark Shaw, *Global Awakening: How 20th Century Revivals Triggered a Christian Revolution* (Downers Grove, Ill.: IVP Academic, 2010), 11.

9. Robert Strand, *The Crossings Treasury of Angel Stories: Contemporary Stories of Angelic Encounters* (Mobile, Ala.: Evergreen Press, 2010), 65.

10. Ibid., 119-21.

11. Trudy Harris, *Glimpses of Heaven: True Stories of Hope and Peace at the End of Life's Journey* (Grand Rapids: Revell, 2008), 19-20.

12. Ibid., 17, 50.

13. Don Piper with Cecil Murphey, *90 Minutes in Heaven* (Grand Rapids: Revell, 2004), 25-28.

14. Ibid., 29-31.

15. Ibid., 33.

16. Edith M. Humphrey, *Ecstasy and Intimacy: When the Holy Spirit Meets the Human Spirit* (Grand Rapids: Wm. B. Eerdmans Publishing Co., 2006), 74.

ACKNOWLEDGMENTS

■ I could not have written this book without the encouragement and support of family, friends, and colleagues. I cannot name all of them, but I would like to acknowledge a few who have offered particular help.

I wrote much of this book during a sabbatical granted by Azusa Pacific University. I would like to thank David Esselstrom, chair of the English Department; David Weeks, Dean of the College of Liberal Arts and Sciences; and Mark Stanton, Provost, for making that sabbatical possible.

A number of people helped with specific content for this book. I would particularly like to thank Liz Leahy, Lynn Maudlin, Shari Holstead, and Harvey Wise for their contributions. Elena Smith also offered some helpful critique of a draft of the book. My conversations with Chris Tansey were helpful during my early thinking about this book.

A group of Christian artists and writers to which I belong, called The Niños, has offered steady prayer support during the writing of this book, and I am grateful for their encouragement and friendship. Several Niños in particular, including Diana Glyer, Mike Glyer, Tom Allbaugh, and Barbara Hayes, have supported me with prayer and friendship.

The Spectrum Sunday School class at Glendora (California) Community Church of the Nazarene has also been a great source of spiritual strength. I have been inspired by the teaching of our pastor, Mike Platter.

I am grateful for the work of the staff of Beacon Hill Press of Kansas City, including, among others, Bonnie Perry, Judi Perry, Barry Russell, and Rachel McPherson.

I am grateful for the guidance and help of my agent, Steve Laube.

The whole idea of writing a book would collapse without the love and support of my family. My wife, Peggy, read drafts of the book and also offered endless love and encouragement. My children, Jacob and Katie, have opened my eyes to seeing the world in a new way, and their own faith in God has strengthened mine.

ABOUT THE AUTHOR

Joseph Bentz is the author of *God in Pursuit: The Tipping Points from Doubt to Faith* (Beacon Hill Press of Kansas City, 2010) and three other books on Christian living. He is also the author of the award-winning novel *A Son Comes Home* and three other novels. Bentz is professor of American literature at Azusa Pacific University, in Azusa, California. He earned a Ph.D. and M.A. in American literature from Purdue University and a B.A. in English from Olivet Nazarene University. He lives with his wife and two children in southern California. More information about his books and speaking is available at his web site, <http://www.joseph bentz.com>. His blog "Life of the Mind and Soul" also appears at that site.

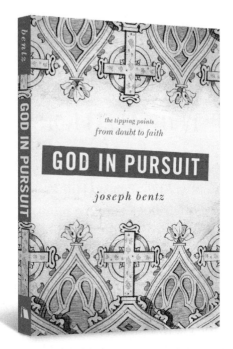

There comes a moment when even the unlikeliest of individuals are drawn into a relationship with Christ.

How does this happen? What is the spark that allows faith to catch fire?

From conversions of cynics who didn't even want to be Christians to Christians whose devotion to Christ is jeopardized due to tragedy, testing, and doubt, *God in Pursuit* examines the dance of doubt and faith. With solid biblical wisdom, author Joseph Bentz helps believers grapple with the crises and questions that can bring us closer to God.

God in Pursuit
The Tipping Points from Doubt to Faith
Joseph Bentz
ISBN 978-0-8341-2492-9

BEACON HILL PRESS
OF KANSAS CITY

Available online and wherever books are sold.